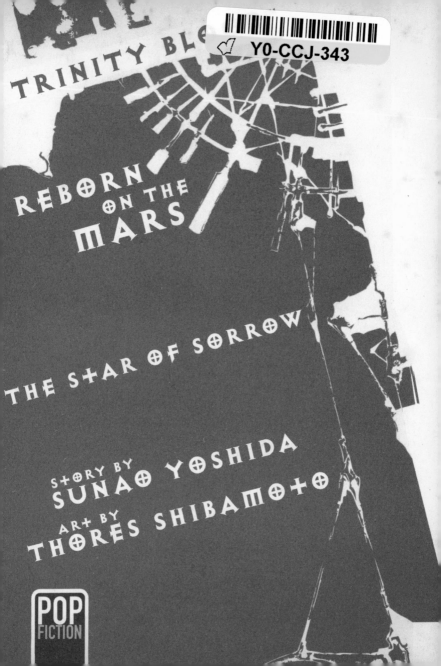

STORY	Sunao Yoshida
ILLUSTRATIONS	THORES Shibamoto
TRANSLATION	Anastasia Moreno
ENGLISH ADAPTATION	Jai Nitz
EDITOR	Kara Stambach
SENIOR EDITOR	Jenna Winterberg
INTERIOR AND	
COVER DESIGN	Jose Macasocol, Jr.
LAYOUT ARTIST	Jennifer Carbajal
PRE-PRESS SUPERVISOR	Erika Terriquez
ART DIRECTOR	Anne Marie Horne
DIGITAL IMAGING MANAGER	Chris Buford
PRODUCTION MANAGER	Elisabeth Brizzi
MANAGING EDITOR	Vy Nguyen
EDITOR-IN-CHIEF	Rob Tokar
VP OF PRODUCTION	Ron Klamert
PUBLISHER	Mike Kiley
PRESIDENT AND COO	John Parker
CEO & CHIEF CREATIVE OFFICER	Stuart Levy

First TOKYOPOP printing: August 2007

10 9 8 7 6 5 4 3 2 1

Printed in the USA

TRINITY BLOOD Reborn on the Mars -THE STAR OF SORROW- © 2001 Sunao Yoshida First published in Japan in 2001 by KADOKAWA SHOTEN PUBLISHING CO., LTD., Tokyo. English translation rights arranged with KADOKAWA SHOTEN PUBLISHING CO., LTD., Tokyo through TUTTLE-MORI AGENCY, INC., Tokyo. English text copyright © 2006 TOKYOPOP Inc.

Library of Congress Cataloging-in-Publication Data
Yoshida, Sunao, d. 2005.
    [Toriniti buraddo. English]
    Trinity blood. The star of sorrow / story by Sunao
Yoshida; art by Thores Shibamoto; translation by Anastasia
Moreno.

    p. cm.
    Audience: age 13-23
    ISBN 978-1-4278-0090-9 (v. 1 : alk. paper)
    I. Shibamoto, Thores. II. Moreno, Anastasia. III. Title.
PN6790.J34T67613 2007   2006028180
741.5'952--dc22

CONTENTS

THE CHARACTERS IN
TRINITY BLOOD
REBORN ON THE MARS

ABEL NIGHTROAD

DIETRICH VON LOHENGRIN

CATERINA SFORZA

ESTHER BLANCHETT

FRANCESCO DI MEDICI

GYULA KADAR

Abel Nightroad—Oddball priest, AX Agent "Crusnik"

Caterina Sforza—Cardinal & Foreign Affairs Minister

Francesco di Medici—Cardinal, Minister of the Vatican Department of Inquisition

Dietrich von Lohengrin—Istavan Partisans Chief of Staff

Esther Blanchett—Novice Sister at Saint Mathias Church

Gyula Kadar—Marquis of Hungary

TRES IQUS

GERGEY RADCON

Tres Iqus—Istavan City Military
Police Major
Gergey Radcon—Istavan City Military
Police Colonel

PROLOGUE:
THE HUNTER'S NIGHT

And surely your blood or your lives will
I require; at the hand of every man's
brother will I require the life of man.
—Genesis 9:5

When the heavy door was pushed open, the pungent odor of blood poured out.

The raw smell wafting from the far end of the church made Sasha cringe, but she determinedly adjusted her grip on the lantern. Her hands were sticky from sweat. The lantern's light flickered weakly, illuminating the surrounding darkness; a festering shadow looked down upon the brave girl.

Sasha had come to this church every week for all her fifteen years, but the church seemed to be wrapped in evil darkness, as if she were a stranger to it.

"Holy Mother Mary, please protect me. Please protect me, Holy Mother Mary," Sasha prayed.

Except for her older brother, Sasha was the bravest soul in the village. The cowardly village residents hid in their homes when "they" arrived. Even her father, the village chief, hid in his home, scattering garlic and mayflowers throughout the estate. No one would aid her brother in getting his fiancée back from them.

Three days ago, Sasha tried to go with her brother to the church where they were, but he refused. He told her to stay home and protect their parents during his absence.

But he didn't return.

"Oh Lord, please protect me. Holy Mother Mary, please protect me," Sasha continued to pray. She took one careful step after another as she scanned the church.

Sasha forced her eyes to stay open without blinking. As she licked her dry lips, she heard the floor creak.

"Wh-who's there?" asked Sasha.

When Sasha pointed her lantern toward the noise, she almost had a heart attack at the sight of a large female figure. After taking three steps back, she finally noticed that the smiling woman holding a baby in her arms was a large marble statue.

Sasha sighed in relief. "P-please don't scare me like that, Holy Mother Mary," she muttered. Her heart still was beating hard, but her knees stopped shaking. She wiped sweat from her cheek. She lightly joked with the village's guardian, the Holy Mother Mary, but when she turned around . . .

This time, Sasha's heart almost stopped.

There were two shadows sitting on the bench.

"Oh, someone is here, Millis," said Malice.

"It's a cute little birdie, Malice," replied Millis.

The two women looked at each other and chuckled. They looked exactly alike—with the same blonde hair and beautiful figures, like alabaster statues. Though it was getting cold enough to snow soon, both of them wore thin, silky dresses. The only difference between the two was the color of their lipstick: one wore light pink, the other dark blue.

Malice, the one with pink lips and amber eyes, spoke. "Millis, what shall we do? We don't have tea to offer her. Where did we put the teapot?"

As the ladies scanned the room and snickered, Sasha thrust her lantern toward them and said, "Wh-where's my brother, you monsters?"

The wavering light from the lantern made the three shadows dance along the walls. Though the shadows made her even more scared, the little girl pulled her strength together and yelled at the top of her lungs, "I-I am Sasha, the daughter of Lord Casprek of Konavri Village! I'm here to avenge my brother's death! I challenge you!"

"Brother? Malice, is that little birdie talking about that brave rooster?" asked Millis. She playfully added, "Remember? The rooster that read the Bible to us?"

With her left hand, Sasha grabbed the rosary hanging from her neck and bellowed, "I-I have a Bible, also! And a cross, too!" Her knees were shaking from fear. Her heart thumped hard.

The two alluring ladies were smiling and talking to each other as if they were singing. But these beautiful women were two of *them*: a new breed born after the Armageddon—an enemy of humankind. They were monsters who were dubbed names like Creatures of the Dark, the Night Clan, Residents of Evil, and so on. The most common name for them was . . .

"Vampires! I'll kill you both!" Sasha declared.

"Little birdie, your brother was delicious," a voice whispered directly into her ear.

When two hands grabbed her shoulders, Sasha's face went pale. The figures that were supposed to be sitting in front of her were no longer there. They had moved behind her almost instantaneously.

The two ladies took turns speaking:

"He read from the Bible feverishly . . ."

"And pointed the cross at us . . ."

"But eventually, he cried for his life . . ."

"And finally, he became our delicious meal."

Sasha was too scared to move as they spoke to her. As she stood frozen from fear, a cold hand squeezed her stiff fingers, making her drop the lantern.

Malice commented, "This little birdie is a bit smarter than her brother, Millis. She's prepared for battle."

"So true, Malice. She brought a lantern made of putrid silver, which is the second-most fatal thing, other than those ultraviolet rays that we hate so much," replied Millis, pursing her dark blue lips as she kicked the lantern toward the far corner of the church.

The candle lost its flame as it fell out of the lantern, and everything went dark.

Long fangs protruded from Millis' blue lips, and she sweetly said, "Don't be scared, little birdie. You'll get to see your beloved brother soon."

Malice added, "Little birdie, I wonder how you taste." As the moonlight shone through the church window, Malice planted her pink lips on the little girl's neck.

The white, glinting fangs slowly sank into Sasha's soft, pale skin.

Just then, a snowy white flash shot through the darkness.

Malice shrieked in pain as she arched back. A plain cross pierced through her hand, the rest of the rosary dangling from the crucifix. The cross itself wasn't sharp, so it must have been thrown at great speed to pierce her hand.

Millis, her lips quivering, held her sister, who writhed in her arms. "Malice!" She glared behind her, enraged, and demanded, "Who's there? Is there yet another village idiot who wishes to disturb our tasty meal . . . ?"

From the ceiling window, two moons shone down. The first moon was a silver sphere, whereas the second moon was a bloody red sphere. A tall figure was illuminated by the eerie moonlight.

"Unfortunately, I'm not a village resident," said the shadowy figure.

"Vampires Malice and Millis Zatrovska . . . In the name of the Father, the Son, and the Holy Spirit, you are under arrest for twenty-two counts of murder, as well as extortion of blood at Konavri Village," the figure continued.

Millis scowled at the figure. "You, in that priest robe!"

The tall man was wearing a black robe and a matching cape. A gold rosary hung from his chest.

"Vatican!" Millis yelled.

He tried to politely say, "Oh, let me introduce myself. I was dispatched from the Vatican Papal State Affairs—" but was interrupted by a bone-crunching sound.

The rosary cross that had pierced the vampire had been stabbed into the priest's back. Millis instantaneously had jumped behind the priest and roared, "How dare you injure me, you lowly Terran?! Die, Vatican pawn!" She forcefully pushed the rosary cross all the way into his body.

His heart thumped unnaturally; he fell to his knees.

Blood spurted from his body and onto Millis' beautiful face, but she just smiled in satisfaction and said, "That was too easy. The priest of this church and this Vatican dog are too weak, don't you think, Malice?"

Malice replied, "It doesn't matter. But please don't mess up the floor, Millis. You need to take care of his blood, okay?" Malice looked down at the little girl in her arms.

The brave "little birdie" had fainted during the traumatic event.

"Well, I'll take care of this little birdie then," said Malice with a laugh as she pushed the little girl's hair away from her white face. *She's pretty for a Terran, so her blood might taste good, too,* Malice thought.

The only sounds heard in the church were teeth piercing flesh, gulps of blood, and sighs of pleasure.

Malice said, "If it tastes that good, please save half for me, Millis." She pushed hair away from the girl's neck. "I'll leave half of this little birdie's blood for you, too."

"Sorry, but I can't let you do that," replied a voice other than her sister's.

The voice continued, "I'm on a restricted diet, so I can't have the girl's blood."

Malice was confused. When she turned around, she saw her sister's eyes gaping open, like a Terran's. Only soft sighs escaped her sister's blue lips, and her face was paler than usual. But what disturbed Malice was not the sight of her sister; rather, it was the tall figure hovering over her.

"Wh–what? No way! Who are you?!" Malice asked, flabbergasted. She saw the man's lips kissing her sister's throat. Red blood trickled down Millis' neck. Malice was accustomed to the sight of blood, but . . .

"No way! H–he's sucking her blood!" Malice sputtered.

The man dropped Millis—who was powerless from fear and blood loss—and sadly asked, "Haven't you ever thought about this?" From his smiling lips, long fangs protruded. "Humans eat cows and chickens. And your kind eats humans. So, who eats your kind?" he asked.

"Oh, I heard that the Vatican, our enemy, keeps a horrible monster. The monster that drinks our blood," Malice replied.

The man slowly approached the frightened vampire. "Yes. I am a Crusnik—a vampire that drinks the blood of other vampires."

CITY OF BLOOD

*Woe to the bloody city! It is all full of
lies and robbery; the prey departeth not.*
—Nahum 3:1

I

The red sunset shone down from the ceiling windows. The bloody red sun was as hard and cold as a witch's kiss.

Abel Nightroad stepped onto the station platform, which was surrounded in steam from the stopped train. He blew out a white cloud of breath. "Wow, it's so cold today," Abel remarked. He pushed his thick glasses up the bridge of his nose as he looked around the empty train station with his winter-blue eyes.

The train station, covered in windows from end to end, was almost as big as a palace, but it was practically vacant, with the exception of a handful of travelers with luggage and a few station attendants who trudged around miserably.

Upon closer examination, though, the train station was not well maintained. Several floor tiles were broken, and some of the windowpanes were cracked.

"This place is a dump. I wonder if I could skip it and just head straight back to Rome," Abel muttered.

The engineer, poking his head out from the train, yelled at the mumbling priest, "Hey, tall man! Why are you still here? Get the hell out! It's dangerous to stay here!"

"Oh, sorry. Um, but . . . may I ask you something? Is this really the last stop?" Abel queried.

"Yeah, of course. That's what that sign says, too," replied the engineer as he pointed to the sign above Abel.

Abel looked at the sign, which had Hungarian and official Roman writing on it.

The engineer read the sign, "This is Istavan—the free capital. Istavan Central Station."

"Oh, I see. I wish it were a mistake, though," Abel commented, running his hands through his scraggly, silver-blond hair.

"With the motto 'The Pearl of the Danube,' I was expecting a glamorous spot, but this is just plain countryside. Don't you think so?" asked Abel.

"Whatever! Just get out of my way! I need to return to Vienna today!" the engineer barked.

The train had just arrived, so Abel asked, "Oh? Leaving already?" He continued, "Um, sir, could you please wait a minute? I was trying to decide whether to return to Rome—knowing that I'd be fired—or stay here . . ."

The engineer scoffed. "Stupid, it'll be night real soon! I don't want to stay here any longer than I have to!"

Abel asked, "Huh? Um, what do you mean—ow!"

The train expelled steam as its whistle blew. Large train wheels rolled past the priest, who stood there in his long coat.

"Th-that's dangerous! You almost burned me alive," Abel said, flustered.

The engineer warned, "See you later, Mister! I suggest you find a lodge and hide for your life. Otherwise . . ."

"Otherwise what?" Abel couldn't hear the rest over the roar of the steam engine. The train switched tracks and disappeared into the blue horizon.

Abel coughed. "Good Lord, my coat is covered in soot," he said, but no one was around to listen to his complaints.

He grabbed his travel bag and dusted off his coat as he walked on the platform. The sky was getting darker by the moment. He needed to find a place to stay before nightfall. But as he hurried, he couldn't dodge another figure dashing out toward him.

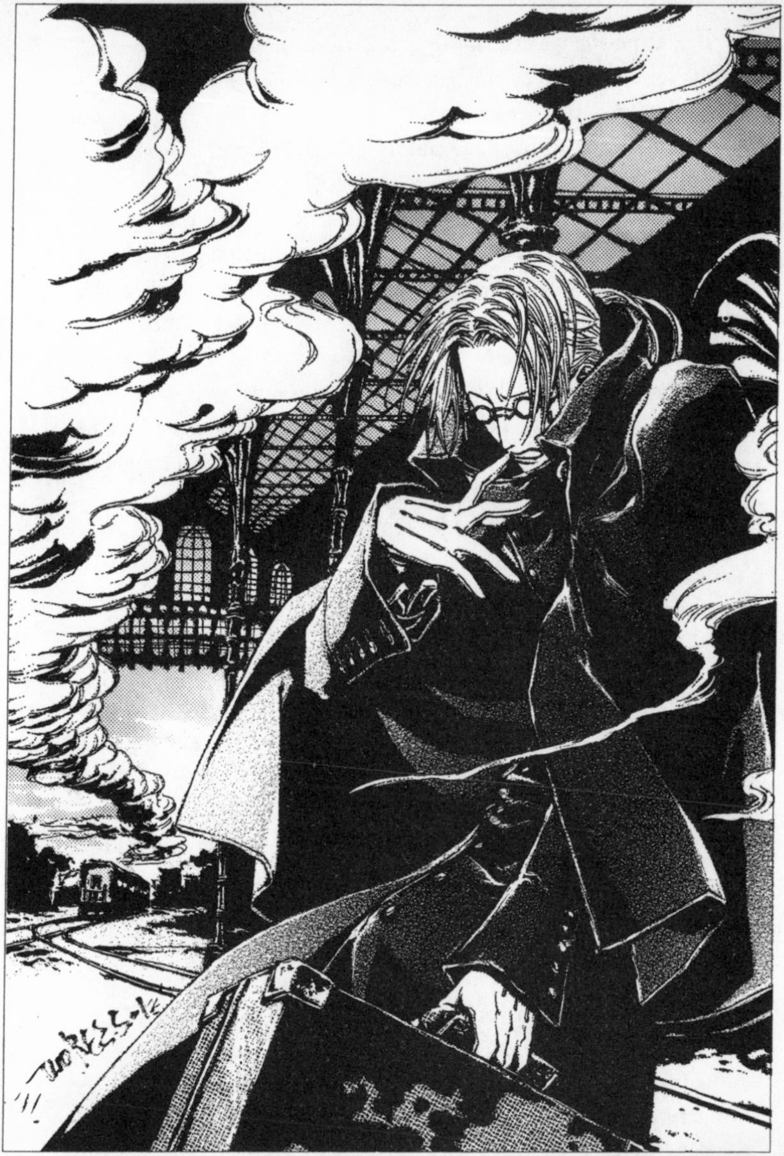

The person yelped, flung a paper bag into the air, and fell down. Something inside the bag cracked as it hit the tile floor.

"S-sorry!" the person apologized.

As Abel was trying to regain his balance, he said, "It's my fault for not paying attention. Are you okay?"

It was a little boy on the ground. "Ow," the boy said as Abel patted his back. The boy was wearing a thick jacket and wool pants. He wore a large scarf wrapped around his neck, and a deerstalker cap covered most of his face. The boy was rather small, only as tall as Abel's chest.

Abel apologized. "I'm so sorry. Are you hurt?"

"D-don't touch me!" The boy swatted Abel's outstretched hand with his skinny arm. The boy patted down his coat and smoothly stood up.

"I'm really sorry," Abel said. "By the way, your bag made a strange sound. Is it okay?"

"Ah . . ." the boy tried to reach for the bag, but Abel beat him to it and picked it up. The bag was quite heavy, and it was soaked at the bottom.

"Is it a bottle of oil?" Abel asked; but when he opened the bag, a stinging odor hit his nose. Inside were two bottles—one with clear fluid and the other with brown. The bottle of clear fluid was cracked, and it drenched the pocket watch tucked at the bottom of the bag.

"Oh, the pocket watch looks broken. The springs are sticking out. I'm sorry; I'll pay for this, too," Abel apologized.

The little boy muttered weakly, "No, it's okay. That watch was broken in the first place." He was trying to step away slowly from Abel. "No need to pay for damages," the boy insisted. "It's not that expensive, anyway. Can you just give it back to me?"

"Eh?" Abel pulled out his wallet. "But I need to properly compensate for your damaged items. How much is it? Will two hundred dinars cover everything? Let's see what I have on me . . . Oh no, I have only eight dinars!" exclaimed Abel. He grabbed the little boy's arm and said, "I'm sorry; I don't have much on me. If you don't mind, can you wait a bit? I promise to pay you."

The boy responded, "S-sure, no problem."

"Great!" Abel was relieved. "Thank you for understanding my situation. If I can have your name and address, I'll—"

"A-address? No, forget it. Don't bother," the boy said.

"No, please let me pay!" Abel persisted. "By the way, I'm Abel Nightroad. I've been transferred here from Rome. Nice to meet you."

The boy was squirming to break free from the priest's grasp. At first, his eyes, which sparkled like lapis lazuli, showed that he was frantic to get away. But as they glanced at the ticket gate, his expression went cold.

About a dozen burly men in uniform were just about to enter the platform. They all wore dark blue coats and berets, but the guns that hung from their hips made it obvious that they weren't train attendants.

Abel blabbered, "Well, Istavan is so quiet. This is my first time here in a poor—I mean, 'solemn'—countryside."

"I-I gotta go," the boy said.

The uniformed men headed straight for them, but Abel continued to ramble.

The boy tried to cut him off. "I've got a few more errands to do. So . . ."

"Oh, is that so? Then please tell me your name and address. I will visit you tomorrow," Abel said.

"No, please forget it," the boy pleaded.

"Hey, you!" a gruff voice interjected. "What the hell are you guys doing here?"

The man who spoke had cloudy eyes and was as big as a bear. He was a tad taller than Abel, and he was twice as thick. He had the stature of a military soldier. A large pistol hung from his hips. The dual-cross badge on his beret was the Istavan city emblem.

Abel asked, "Uh, who are you?"

"I am Colonel Gergey Radcon—Istavan City Military Police," the man with small, cruel eyes replied.

His grubby hand rested on his gun's holster. He didn't look like he had many friends, so the other men behind him must have been his subordinates.

"Don't you know that this train station is off-limits after eighteen hundred hours every day? What the hell are you guys doing?" Radcon asked.

"Uh, well, I dropped the bag that this boy had been holding. I was trying to pay for the damages. I'm really sorry for causing trouble," Abel bashfully replied.

Radcon glared at the two with his beady eyes, but he let his guard down after seeing Abel's apologetic gestures. He snorted and motioned with his chin. "Get the hell outta here."

"O-oh, we can go? Thank you, thank you." Abel bowed repeatedly. "Well then—whoa!" His legs tangled and he fell facedown onto the ground with a yelp.

"Hey, don't destroy the train station, now." Radcon laughed. The men behind him laughed, as well.

"Ow." Abel touched his red nose. Blood trickled down between his fingers.

"Hey, are you all right?" the boy asked as he kneeled down and handed Abel a tissue. "Use this. Can you stand?"

Abel grabbed at the tissue and clumsily stood up with the boy's help.

"Be careful. Walk slowly," the boy advised.

"Thank you. I'm so careless," Abel remarked.

As Abel leaned on the boy's shoulder to walk, Radcon called out, "Hey, slinky!" The two looked back. "Don't fall again, huh!"

Radcon taunted them in a condescending manner, and his men roared with laughter. Radcon rubbed his chin as he made a few more lewd comments. His group continued to laugh as they walked away.

The boy muttered, "Thugs." Unfortunately, his comment was heard despite the uproar.

The men stopped laughing and looked at their superior officer's face.

"Wait." Radcon swiftly grabbed the boy's shoulder with his thick hands and asked, "What'd you say? You calling us 'thugs'?"

The boy remained silent.

Before the boy could shake his shoulder or swat at Radcon's big arm, he was slammed to the ground. Luckily, he broke his fall like a martial artist; but before he could stand back up, Radcon pulled him up by the collar.

Radcon growled. "What makes you think you can call a City Military Police colonel a 'thug,' huh?!"

His thick upper arm was grayish in color, which indicated that Radcon probably was an "enhanced soldier" from the Germanic Kingdom or Franc.

He was one of the lost technologies that was salvaged—an enhanced soldier from before the Armageddon, biologically engineered to be as strong as a bear.

The other soldiers made complaints such as "Oh man, he's at it again," and "He has such a short temper," as well as "Colonel, don't injure them too much." They must have been used to his bursts of rage.

The train attendants, afraid of what was brewing, hid in the shadows.

"Hey, say something! Or are you too afraid to talk? You're such a spineless coward," Radcon scoffed. Radcon shook the boy and smiled. "You called me a 'thug.' You'd better take responsibility for your comment."

The boy, struggling for breath, replied, "Screw you. I just spoke the truth."

"Hah! Brave fellow, hm?" Radcon scrunched up his face for a moment. He peered under the deerstalker cap and asked, "Hey you, don't tell me . . . ?"

Radcon slapped the cap off the boy's head. Red hair that had been stuffed into the deerstalker cap tumbled out. Radcon smiled slyly when he saw the little white face. "Well, damn! I got me a pretty one!" Radcon sneered.

The "boy" turned out to be a pale-faced young girl in her early teens. She didn't have on any makeup, but her sparkling blue eyes and distinct facial features displayed the kind of beauty that would make any man look twice.

She bit into her thin lower lip out of pain and humiliation.

"Hey, look at her! This one's a beauty!" Radcon grinned. "We'll enjoy this one for a *long* time, fellas!"

The men made lewd comments.

"Oh man, Colonel Radcon's bad habit started again."

"Poor little girl. She won't be going home to her family tonight."

"Colonel, please keep her in one piece after you're done with her."

As Radcon showed off his prize, he brought his nasty face close to hers and asked, "What's your name, little lady?"

"Esther—Esther Blanchett," she replied.

"Good, that's a good name. Esther, let's get to know each other, okay? And once I take care of business tonight, I'll treat you real good," Radcon said.

"No!" Esther slapped Radcon's cheek, despite that he held her up in midair.

"Let go of me, you thug! If you let me go, I'll let things slide. If not, I won't let you get away with this!" Esther barked at the giant, who was twice her height and three times as thick. She had no chance of winning. In this case, her courage probably would make things worse.

"What a strong wench—" Radcon rubbed his reddened cheek as his men watched in amusement. "Just my type of girl."

Esther was thrown into a column, and she crumpled to the ground like a broken doll. "O-ooof!"

"I usually have dessert *after* work, but . . ." Radcon pushed her, his thick fingers reaching for her collar. "I'll have you now!"

Esther tried to resist, but he ripped open her clothes, exposing her white skin. Radcon's placed his big hand on her small breasts.

Her thin legs kicked around in vain.

"S-stop it!" the girl protested.

"Shut up! You'll feel good in no time!" Radcon licked the girl's flushed face; he especially enjoyed when girls resisted like this.

"S-stop it, you imbecile!" she screamed.

"Oh yeah, I really like a strong bitch like you," he muttered.

Esther's screams echoed through the train station, but no one tried to save her.

The more Esther fought, the more pleasure Radcon felt. He was just about to unzip his pants when . . .

"Excuse me?" an awkward voice interjected. It completely stopped the giant from laughing and the girl from screaming.

"Sorry to interrupt you, but may I ask a question?" the awkward voice continued.

"What? You're still here?" growled Radcon, raising his half angry, half lusty red face.

It was the bespectacled young priest. Abel looked down upon the giant and the girl underneath him and said, "Um, I broke her bottle, so I was trying to ask for her name and address so I could repay her."

"Stupid, run away!" the girl squealed.

"Hey, hold her while I take care of this idiot," Radcon ordered.

Radcon slowly stood up while his men held down Esther's arms and legs. He glared like an angry bear at Abel.

"Eh?" Abel blinked.

Radcon stared into his face, but Abel coughed and said in a serious voice, "Um, the Lord hath said, 'Thou shall not commit adultery.'"

"Hmph!" Radcon punched Abel's face, knocking him to the ground. Radcon sneered. "I like to overpower girls and make them writhe, but I also like making men scream like little girls when I beat them to a pulp."

Abel was on all fours, coughing; Radcon stomped on his back and grasped Abel's silver hair. The priest was too strained for words.

"S-stop it!" Esther shrieked.

Radcon kept his foot on Abel's back and forcefully bent the man in two as he pulled up Abel's silver hair and arm. Abel's arching spine was starting to strain.

"Stop it! He has nothing to do with this!" Esther pleaded.

"How far can he go?" Radcon grinned. He pulled Abel's head and arm until Abel's eyes rolled up.

"Please stop! He'll die!" Esther yelled.

"Don't worry. He'll only break his back and be paralyzed for life," Radcon joked. He thoroughly enjoyed Abel's strain. After a moment, Radcon pulled harder and remarked, "All right, he's almost done."

"I recommend you end it here, Colonel Radcon," said a cold, steely voice. A gloved hand tapped Radcon's shoulder. "Colonel, our section has left our post vacant for more than four hundred and seventy-eight seconds. Request to return to our posts, sir."

"What?" Radcon replied in disgust. He looked behind him and blurted, "Tres Iqus!"

Radcon looked up to see an emotionless man. He seemed to be in his early twenties. There was the shiny rank insignia for major on the collar of his neatly pressed uniform.

"Major Iqus! Are you trying to interrupt a superior officer?" Radcon barked.

"Negative. I do not intend to interrupt your recreational pursuits, sir," replied Tres. He answered in an emotionless but succinct manner. "But I regret to inform you that we are still on duty. I recommend you pursue your pleasure after duty. As of eighteen hundred twenty-seven hours, the only area that is not secure yet is your section," Iqus reported.

"Iqus, are you talking down to me, by Almighty God? Don't act too big just because you're Gyula's favorite," Radcon huffed at the clean-cut face. "Gyula ain't coming for at least an hour. I can secure my area in less than thirty minutes. Butt out, you idiot!"

"We received transmission that the special train will arrive thirty minutes earlier," Tres stated.

"What?!" sputtered Radcon as he scrunched up his face.

"Lord Gyula will arrive at nineteen hundred hours—it is now twenty seconds past that time. Colonel, I recommend that you secure your area immediately," Tres warned.

"Dammit!" Radcon let go of Abel's head, which dropped to the ground with a loud *thud*. Radcon kicked Abel's side; then he turned around in disgust.

He yelled to his men, "Hey, what are you guys looking at? Get in position!" He glared at the young, emotionless major. As his men scrambled to their posts, Radcon added, "Oh, before I forget, you guys drag that tall moron over here! Once we take care of business, we'll take him to the Valley of Blood. I'll interrogate him real good."

"No! He didn't do anything wrong!" Esther protested as she fixed her clothes. Though she hadn't been afraid even when she was about to be raped, she definitely was frightened at the thought of Abel's impending predicament. "You can't send him to the Valley of Blood! He didn't commit any crime!"

"Shut up! If you keep it up, I'll drag you out there, too—for charges of violence against City Military Police, interference of official duties, destruction of public property . . . you name it. We can add spy charges, too. Major Iqus, you have no objections, right?" Radcon inquired.

"Positive. Enforce as you please," Tres responded.

"Great, will do." Radcon cackled. He motioned to his men and ordered, "Take them away!"

II

Though the sun had set, there should have been a few more trains arriving that night. The train station should have been full of travelers coming and going.

But the station did not have any passengers or attendants when a train without windows stopped abruptly, making a sound like a demon's nails scratching against metal. Instead, a formation of military personnel stood in dark blue uniforms, rifles at their shoulders.

They were expressionless, looking more like dolls than humans. Yet there was almost a sense of fear from the group when the train completely stopped.

The leader ordered, "Present arms!"

The soldiers raised their rifles in salute. The bayonets gleaned from the dull light of the gas lamps.

The train blew steam onto the platform, turning the long line of soldiers' breaths into white clouds.

"Welcome back," Radcon said, greeting the lone passenger as he disembarked. Radcon showed no signs of the disgust that he'd displayed moments before. He bowed down so low that his beret almost touched the deck. "Lord Gyula, you must be tired from the long trip, sir."

"Good job, Colonel," a handsome young man wearing a cape commented.

The tall young man had a nicely featured white face, contrasted by jet-black hair; the overall effect matched the grayness of the town. His eyes were like that of a werewolf—gray with black pupils—and they seemed darker than night, with an eerie gleam that would unnerve anyone.

As he raised the collar of his cape, the young noble asked in a low voice, "Did anything happen in Istavan during my absence?"

"Sir, there were a few Partisans who caused trouble, but we subdued them. We transported the leader to the Valley of Blood; so please rest assured, things have been taken care of," Radcon replied.

The giant acted more like a slave than a faithful servant. But Gyula just nodded at Radcon's overly polite report and walked along the wall of soldiers standing on the platform.

"How was the Empire, Lord Gyula?" asked Radcon.

"Stubborn as usual: They refused to provide assistance for my plan. And I wasn't able to meet Empress Augusta. But once they see the massive power of *that*, I'm sure they will change their minds," Gyula remarked. The nobleman cracked a small smile. His handsome expression—or perhaps his fangs—added to the cruel effect.

"The hardware was recovered. After we test the software, we should be able to conduct a test fire. By the way, who is that?" Gyula asked about the silver-haired man who stood among the men in uniform with his hands bound.

"He is a suspicious person who made unfavorable comments about City Military Police, sir. We subdued him and plan to interrogate him later," Radcon replied.

"Hmm." Gyula almost walked past the silver-haired man; but then he turned and asked, "Excuse me. What's your name?"

"Abel . . . Abel Nightroad," Abel replied. His face was black and blue from the beating, and his lips were cut. "I came from Rome. I was transferred here from the Vati—"

Radcon grabbed Abel's collar, causing one of the buttons to pop. He growled, "Stop blabbing. Answer only his questions, nothing more."

Gyula softly interjected, "Now hold on, Colonel." Underneath the tattered coat, he saw a rosary and Abel's outfit. "A rosary and a priest's robe . . . Are you a priest?"

"Y-yes. I have been assigned to work at the Saint Mathias Church in Istavan," Abel replied with pain in his voice, as Radcon kept grasping his collar. "I haven't done—"

"I said shut up!" Radcon barked.

"Colonel, you be quiet. Let go of the priest," Gyula ordered.

"B-but, sir!" Radcon protested.

"Did you not hear me, Colonel? Let go of the priest *now*," Gyula firmly repeated.

Radcon shuddered at his superior's change in tone.

"I do not pay attention to—or rather, I do not care about your personal pursuits. But I cannot tolerate servants who do not listen to my commands. Understood?" Gyula emphasized.

"I-I'm very sorry, sir!" Radcon lowered his head.

Gyula ignored Radcon and looked back at Abel. He politely bowed to Abel, who was rubbing his strained neck. "Pardon me. I am Gyula Kadar. I am a merchant in this city. I apologize for the misunderstanding my men had with you. On behalf of the people of Istavan, I offer my sincere apologies," Gyula said.

"Oh, thank you for your kind apology." Abel bowed his head in response.

Though Abel was tall, bespectacled, and had silver hair, he seemed to be a normal young man. But there was something about him. Had Gyula met him before? "Excuse me, Father, but have I met you before?" Gyula inquired.

"No, I've never been to this town before," Abel answered.

"Oh . . . well, this place is just a lonely rural area compared to Rome, but please enjoy your stay here." Gyula chuckled and reached out for a handshake. Gyula was convinced he'd never met the priest and decided to end the conversation. "Welcome to Istavan, Father Nightroad. We're happy to have you here."

"Uh, thank you," Abel replied as he shook Gyula's hand.

Gyula saw Abel's face go white, so he wondered if he had gripped the man's hand a bit too hard; but he finally noticed that Abel was looking at something behind him. By then, however, Abel's thin arms had powerfully pushed Gyula to the ground.

"Wh-what are you doing, you moron?!" Radcon roared as he ran toward his lord and the priest. But something zipped in front of him and cut him short.

A small metal rod had flown over Gyula's head and clanged into the train. The rod was as thick as a finger and had strange fins at its base.

"Arrows!" a soldier tried to warn the others, but an arrow pierced his shoulder and took him down. Next to him, another soldier tried to fire back but was hit by a shot to his stomach.

Suddenly, gunfire illuminated the night.

Molotov cocktails surrounded them. As the flaming bottles flew toward the platform, some of the soldiers were shot down before they could react.

"Enemy attack! It's the Partisans!"

Where had they been hiding? A countless number of capped and ski-masked men appeared, holding lit flare balls.

"Spread out! Fire back at will!" Radcon ordered, but the enemy fired at a coordinated pace.

The Molotov cocktails cracked onto the platform upon impact and spread gasoline and fire. The random fires lit the platform like a theatrical stage.

"Everyone, forget the pawns! Go for Gyula! Gyula!" a high-pitched voice called out.

Thick arrows flew out from the same direction as before. One of the arrows scathed Abel's cheek and buried into the metal pillar behind him. The arrows were tipped with silver nitrate, which left a pungent odor on Abel's cheek.

"O-oh yeah, my pistol! Where did I put my pistol?" Abel fished in his pockets.

"Please get down, Father," Gyula said, pushing Abel's head down as he stood up and took off his cape. He shook his cape like a bullfighter, using it to swat the arrows coming his way. But the archers that shot with precision were still more impressive.

When Gyula noticed that the arrows were coming from the last cab of the train on the opposite platform, he grinned.

"Colonel!" Gyula called.

"Yes, sir!" Radcon replied.

Though Gyula's military suffered losses in the initial stage of the ambush, his soldiers effectively took cover and fired back. The archers continued their barrage, but they were not as effective without the element of surprise. Even the Molotov cocktails were now shot down in midair, helping expose the enemy's position.

"It seems to be only a small number of enemies. Have some of your men flank the left side and surround them," Gyula ordered.

"Roger that, sir! Major Iqus, flank on the left and surround them!" Radcon ordered.

"Affirmative," replied Tres. He took several of his men toward the other platform. The enemy noticed their movements, and they threw fewer Molotov cocktails.

Radcon yelled, "I won't let you escape, Partisans!" as he pointed his large pistol.

One archer continued to shoot arrows at the same pace, providing cover fire for his retreating comrades. Radcon aimed toward the origin of the attack and fired.

Someone cried out. A small figure, holding a lever-action crossbow, grabbed its shoulder and crouched over. One of the Partisans called out, "Are you okay, Star?!"

Holding a submachine gun, the Partisan ran to the archer; but upon seeing the wound, he said, "This operation is a failure. I'll cover for you. Go, Star!"

The small figure in the ski mask protested, but gunfire muffled its argument.

The Partisan yelled out, "Stupid! We can't let our leader die! I'll hold them here. Get away with the others!"

The City Military Police increased their fire. Another squad of Partisans that had been standing by outside the train station noticed the change in the situation and so came to assist. The archer named Star was silent at first; but eventually, a nod and a whistle signalled the attackers to retreat into the darkness.

"Heh! You're not getting away, terrorists!" Radcon gruffed. He aimed at the retreating leader's small back. "Die!"

"Found it!" Abel cried out as he pulled out a rather old percussion revolver from his chest pocket. He pulled the hammer back and pulled the trigger haphazardly.

"Hah, hah, now I can help out! You're not getting away terrorists . . . huh?"

There was a dull click and a puff of white smoke.

The percussion struck the gunpowder stuffed inside the round itself. The gunpowder seemed to have been moist, causing a cloud of white smoke, obstructing the officers' view.

"Wh–what the hell?!" Radcon uttered, coughing.

"S–sorry! I'm so sorry!" Abel apologized.

"Did you cause this, you stupid priest?" Radcon growled.

"Wait, Star is getting away!" a soldier called out as Star's comrades provided cover for an escape. A few soldiers fired back, but the smoke screened their view to prevent further battle.

By then, the fight was nearly over.

Around them were the injured and dead. The gunfire gradually ceased. Several soldiers yelled out:

"Check for damages!"

"Transport the injured!"

"Don't kill the captured suspects. Arrest them for interrogation!"

With tears in his eyes, Gyula asked, the coughing priest, "Are you okay, Father? I must thank you for saving my life."

"Oh, gosh. But who were those people? Your men called them Partisans or something?" asked Abel.

"They're putrid terrorists that live in this town!" Radcon grudgingly answered. "With their leader, Star, they assassinate VIPs, destroy public property, and commit other heinous acts! A bunch of rotten scoundrels!"

"Hey, keep walking!" a soldier barked at one of the arrested Partisans, whose hands were bound above his head. It was the one who had spoken with Star.

"Oh, good evening, terrorist," Gyula said politely, though his face, covered in dirt and blood, was twisted in a grim expression. He looked down at the terrorist's bound hands and feet to remark, "Thank you for the hearty welcome. Your bunch is always so lively."

"You monster!" the terrorist yelled. He bit into his swollen lip, glaring with rage at the handsome Gyula. "How dare you fester in our city?! Because of you, this city—"

Radcon kicked him in the gut. "Be quiet, you disrespectful fool!"

The terrorist doubled over in pain. Blood and spittle dripped from his mouth onto the platform.

"How dare you speak to Lord Gyula like that?!" Radcon barked.

"Enough, Colonel. He's injured." Gyula stopped Radcon before Abel could speak out. "If you work him up too much, he won't be able to answer our questions. . . . Oh, have someone take the priest to his new church before it gets too late."

"Uh, you don't need to do that. . . ." Abel shook his head and tried to politely turn down the offer, but Gyula waved his hand.

"Don't worry. After all, you saved my life. Major Iqus, get the car ready and escort him," Gyula directed.

"Affirmative. This way, Father Nightroad," Tres ordered tonelessly.

Before Abel walked off, however, Gyula called out as if he remembered something, "Oh, Father. I have a question. . . . Before transferring here, what was your job in Rome?" Gyula asked.

"Oh, I was in charge of a small church, but they suddenly transferred me here, so I came unprepared. I'm not sure what I did wrong, though. Maybe the cardinal saw me lecturing a road sign when I was a little too drunk." Abel responded.

"I see," Gyula said. He'd noticed a brief pause before the priest answered his question. Gyula continued, "I apologize for asking such a random question. My men will escort you to your new church, so please take care."

"Yes, thank you." Abel bowed and left.

Gyula stood on the platform and watched until Abel left the train station. After a while, Gyula noticed the Partisan crouched on the ground at his feet. "Oh, that's right. I haven't heard your story yet," he stated.

The terrorist didn't have time to open his mouth. A graceful hand grabbed the terrorist's chin and lifted him up into the air. "What were you calling me? A monster, right?" Gyula asked.

"Ah, ah, ah . . ." the terrorist stuttered. An inhumanly powerful arm lifted him. The terrorist's eyes were filled with fear, the look of a death row inmate before his impending execution.

The noble grinned, his fangs poking out from the side. Gyula craned toward the terrorist's neck.

"D–don't!" the terrorist's scream stopped in mid-sentence, because Gyula had planted his fangs into the man's neck. Red blood trickled down onto the platform.

Gyula sighed and looked up at the man's bulging eyes. The terrorist was as white as a marble statue. When Gyula released his grasp, the man's body crumpled limply to the ground like a broken doll.

"He had a lot of blood in him, but it didn't taste good. I want to taste Star's blood for a comparison," Gyula commented.

The terrorist continued to convulse slightly.

"Hmph, you lowly Terran. Claiming this town as yours. This is *my* town. Colonel!" Gyula called out.

"Y-yes, sir!" Radcon replied as he broke through the ranks of his men, pale and sweaty from the horrendous sight.

As Gyula wiped his mouth, he ordered, "Have one of your informants check that priest's background. There's something suspicious about him."

"Roger that, sir!" Radcon held back his comments and saluted. Behind him, soldiers were clearing out the dead bodies. Gyula saw the fear in their eyes as he took swift steps out of the train station.

"Damn Vatican! Did they find out something already?" Gyula wondered.

Gyula hadn't heard of any personnel shortages at the Saint Mathias Church, and the timing of a new priest coming to town right before the final preparation was too coincidental.

The Vatican cannot stop me, but I should get rid of as many negative variables as possible, Gyula thought. *It's probably good to give the informant a heads up. But if that priest is one of the Vatican's agents, then . . .*

Well, we'll deal with it then, Gyula thought.

The priest probably tasted good. The young lord licked his lips with his pointy tongue.

III

Welcome to Istavan, Father Nightroad. I am Bishop Laura Vitez; I'm in charge of this church," said Vitez.

"Nice to meet you." Abel cracked a clumsy grin at the thirty-year-old woman seated at the desk.

Religious books lined the walls of the church and loomed over the tall priest.

"I heard that something happened at the train station. But as long as you're in this church, you are under the Lord's protection." Vitez made the sign of a cross, but Abel could only twitch.

Saint Mathias Church was a gothic chapel, with high walls surrounding it. The church originally was located on the west side of the river; but after the Armageddon, it was relocated and restored. Though it was a very peaceful building, Abel wasn't able to calm down after that vicious firefight. He felt that he needed something more than the Lord's protection—perhaps alcohol—to live calmly in a rough town like this.

"What's the matter, Father Nightroad? Your face looks quite pale," said Vitez.

"Uh, sorry. I guess I'm relieved—but tired," Abel replied.

"Oh my, I'm sorry I didn't notice that. Someone will take you to your room, so please have a good night's rest. Are you there, Sister Esther?" Vitez called out.

"Yes, Bishop," a clear voice replied from behind Abel. Its owner pranced into the bishop's office.

"Did you call for me, ma'am?" Esther asked.

"Please take Father Nightroad to his room. Once you do that, you can retire to your quarters, too," Vitez ordered.

"Yes, ma'am. Come this way, Father Nightroad. I'll show you to your room," Esther said.

Abel turned and was shocked.

The fact that she was a small, young sister in her teens didn't surprise him. It was what rested under the blue hood that took him by surprise—red hair and a pretty white face.

"Y-you were at the train station!" Abel exclaimed.

"We meet again, Father. Thanks for helping this afternoon." Esther smiled, offering to shake his hand.

It was the girl with the deerstalker cap. Of course, she was no longer wearing boys' clothes; rather, she was clad in a blue novice's gown with a hood trimmed in white.

"You already know Father Nightroad, Esther?" asked Vitez.

"Yes, I met him downtown while I was running errands. He helped me when I got tangled up with the City Military Police. Thank you so much, Father Nightroad. I am Esther Blanchett, a novice," Esther introduced herself.

"What a coincidence. I didn't know you were a nun," Abel remarked as he shook her hand and stared at Esther's face.

He hadn't noticed earlier, but she was indeed a very beautiful girl. Unlike the glum residents of the town, who were typically dark-haired and dark-skinned, she had very distinct facial features. Her eyes sparkled intelligently, reminding him of lapis lazuli. She had a small mouth underneath her well-shaped nose, hinting of a noble background; but possibly, she was from a foreign country—Albion, perhaps.

"Um, is there something on my face?" Esther asked.

"Ah? N-no! There's nothing!" Abel shook his head.

Esther looked at Abel like he was a strange creature; then she said, "Let me show you to your room. Do you have any luggage?"

"Thank you. Have a good evening, Bishop," Abel said.

"Have a good night, Father Nightroad," Vitez said.

"Yes, good night . . . I'm lucky to be spending the night under the same roof as such a cute girl," Abel remarked quietly.

He followed Esther down the hallway, forgetting his hunger and the previous, fearful incident. *A lot of things happened today, but it should be fun tomorrow. The bishop is nice, the air is clean, and the girl is cute. Istavan is a good city, after all.*

"Here we are. This is your room, Father," Esther said.

"Wow, what a . . . room." Abel deflated like a balloon.

The candles illuminated a small, coffinlike room. The only furniture was a small bed that Abel would have to bend his neck and hug his knees to fit on. There was also a small pocket of space that was supposed to be a closet. The ceiling was low, and there were mysterious black stains on the walls that looked almost like a human face. Hanging from the window was a rag for a curtain.

"Um, did you possibly come to the wrong room by mistake?" Abel asked.

"Isn't this a great room? When we heard that an elite priest was going to come from Rome, we prepared this room just for you. Please enjoy it!" Esther gleefully said.

"Thank you." Abel grinned sarcastically.

I can't be depressed about this, Abel thought. *They say "When in Rome, do as the Romans do." I must not let this bother me, though; it may be a prank on newly arrived guests,* he thought.

"We wake up at four o'clock. Morning prayers begin at four thirty, so please don't be late getting to the church. Please put your dirty clothes in the bathroom hamper with your name on it," Esther said.

"Er, Esther, may I ask you something?" Abel said as he sat on the bed.

"Yes, what is it?" Esther tilted her head. Her red hair, neatly tucked into her hood, shimmered in the candlelight.

"When we met at the train station, why were you dressed like that?" Abel asked.

"Dressed? You mean like a boy? It's safest to dress like that in town," Esther replied.

"Safest?" Abel questioned.

"Yes. The town has been getting more violent every day, so it's very dangerous for a woman to walk around alone. That's my camouflage," Esther answered.

"I see. That makes sense." Abel folded his arms and nodded. "Well, I was caught in the middle of a gunfight with the Partisans. That was really scary. And that person called Star sprayed shots like a wild man. I could've been killed."

"Partisans? You were lucky to escape without injuries," Esther remarked.

"Well, I wasn't hurt, but I was really scared," Abel sighed.

Esther stayed silent.

Abel continued, "I think I might have come to a really dangerous place. I'm surrounded by desolate countryside, and the town is violent. My boss and the personnel department really tricked me. Do you suppose I made yet another bad choice by coming here?"

"Uh, do you always make bad choices?" Esther asked.

"In my case, yes. My former boss was very cold and demanding, a bullish monster. I broke down in tears many times. But your boss seems to be a very nice lady," Abel commented.

"Bishop Vitez? Yes, she is very nice." Esther clutched her rosary and proudly boasted about the bishop. "She has been really nice to me since I was young, almost like a mother."

"Since you were young?" Abel inquired.

"Yes, I was raised in this church," Esther replied.

Is Esther an orphan? Abel wondered to himself.

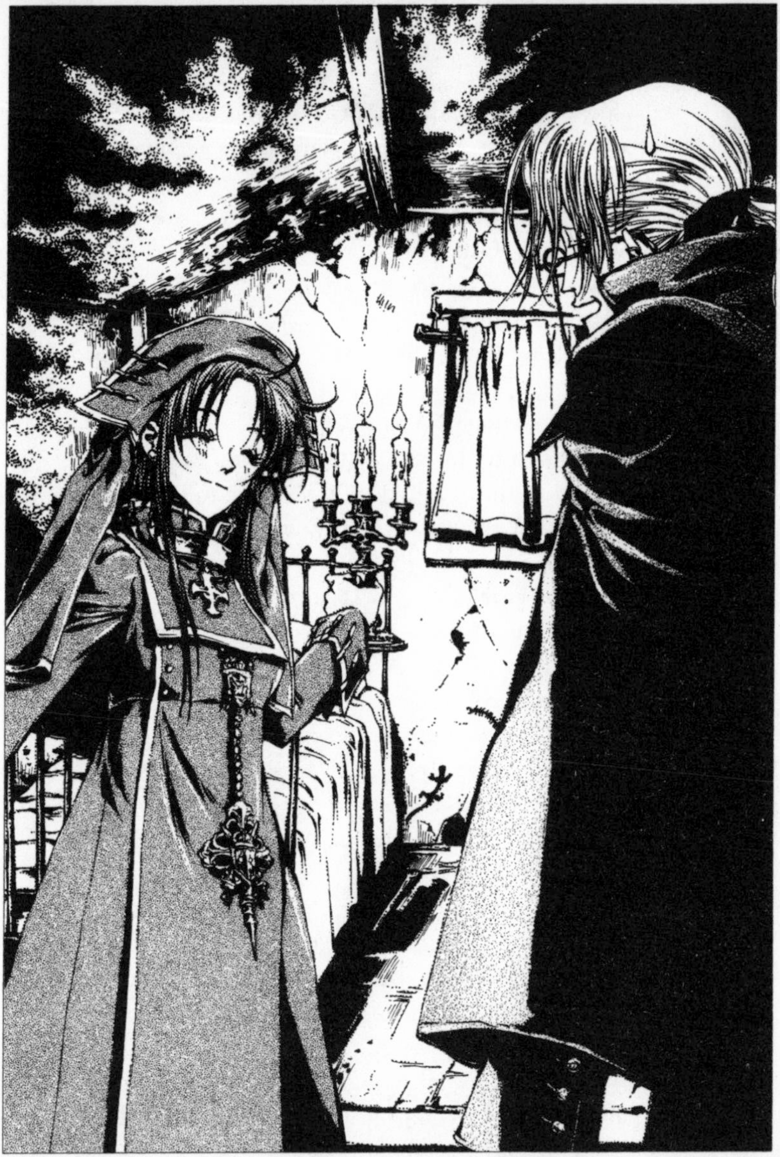

"Oh no! Look at the time!" Esther said as she peered out the window at the clock tower.

She stood up abruptly. Nine o'clock wasn't late for most folks; but with the chapel's early morning schedule, it was definitely past their bedtime.

"I will come wake you tomorrow morning. Please use the blankets to stay warm," Esther said.

"Thank you," Abel replied.

When Abel stood up to see Esther out, Vitez knocked on the door and asked, "Um, Father Nightroad? May I speak with you for a moment?"

"Bishop, what's wrong?" Abel asked.

Vitez said, "I'm sorry to bother you before you sleep, but—"

"Outta the way, Bishop." Radcon pushed her to the side.

Esther gulped at the size of the giant whose head almost touched the ceiling.

"Hey, we meet again, little girl." Radcon sneered.

Esther took a step back as Radcon lustfully looked at her with his beady eyes.

"Why are you here?" Esther cried out.

"Whoa. I'm not gonna play with you tonight, little girl. I'm here for the priest," Radcon replied.

"Huh? Me?" Abel blinked.

Radcon nodded, "Lord Gyula wants to see you tonight. Get ready. He wants you to join him for dinner."

"Lord Gyula? At this time of night? We just saw each other a few minutes ago! Why the sudden request?" Abel asked.

"Hell if I know. We have a car waiting outside. Hurry up," Radcon gruffed.

"Oh." Abel groaned.

"Um!" Esther interjected. She grabbed the priest as he was trying to stand up from his bed. "It's already late, so you shouldn't wander out."

"Nope, that won't do." Radcon shook his head, exposing his rotten teeth. "As long as you're a resident of this city, you can't refuse an invitation to the Valley of Blood. Period."

"There are no regulations like that. And besides, Father just came to town today, so he's not even a resident yet!" Esther pleaded.

"Either way, it's not up to you whether he goes, little girl," Radcon stated. "So, are you coming, Father?"

"If I decline, will something happen to me?" Abel asked.

"Nope. Nothing will happen to you." Radcon leaned back. "I'm a gentleman, too. But starting tomorrow, the people of this church might not be too comfortable."

"What do you mean by that?" Abel persisted.

"The town has been getting more violent these days. Windows get broken, things get stolen, and sisters get taken into alleys."

"Father, we'll be fine. You shouldn't—" Esther insisted.

"Ah, I'll go." Abel nodded. He looked at Esther and said, "I shouldn't decline such an invitation, so I'll go."

"Father!" Esther cried out.

"Good. You get the point." Satisfied, Radcon walked off. The soldiers in the hallway grabbed Abel's arms.

"Well, see ya later. Sorry to bother you while you guys were flirting, but I'll come back and take *good* care of you another time, little girl." Radcon's eyes raked over Esther.

Abel, held by the soldiers, said, "It's going to be all right, Esther. He won't eat me or anything like that. I'll be back tomorrow. Please save my breakfast. Bishop, I'll be back soon," Abel continued.

"See you, Bishop. This church is full of hot chicks. I'll be back again, for sure." Radcon sneered. The men disappeared down the hallway, but Esther remained for a while.

Even after the other clergy retired to their own quarters, Esther remained standing in the hallway, biting her lower lip and looking out the window. "He doesn't know what he got himself into. Father said 'he won't eat me,' but that's exactly what could happen to him at that estate!" Esther grumbled.

Esther turned around, sighing in worry and anger.

IV

No one could explain where they came from, nor why they existed. One theory stated they were a forgotten breed, resurrected from the darkness. Another said a group of people had been afflicted with a certain disease, which caused the changes that created them.

A Vatican-approved book stated that, after the Armageddon, they came from the second moon, claiming they were a totally different species from those found on Earth.

Nobody knew the real reason for their existence.

But it was true that they appeared after the Armageddon—a war involving nuclear and biological weapons that almost wiped out mankind as it destroyed technology that had been developed over hundreds of years, along with large amounts of land. Initially, with their superhuman skills and strength, the humans could not counter their power.

If the Vatican had not pulled together humankind as one and hadn't protected those humans with unusual powers that could only be explained as "God's gift," then they would have dominated humans by now. As a result, in the conflict between humans and the others, the humans prevailed. After several hundred years as interlopers, they retreated back into their own darkness in shame, and the humans slowly and peacefully rebuilt the world after the destruction of the Dark Ages.

Peacefully?

Was it really that peaceful?

It has been more than five hundred years since they retreated into the darkness. But why were people still nervous at night, afraid of things coming out of the shadows? And why were the Crusaders from the east still aggressively protesting at the Pope's palace?

The fight continued.

Based on their unique characteristics and human folklore, the humans called the enemy "vampires."

"The free city, Istavan. Geographically, it is east of Rome and just west of the border of the Empire," a sweet voice announced as the image of the city glowed.

The city was full of domed roofs and columns. A bridge connected the west province, Buda, with the east province, Pest. This beautiful town used to be called "The Pearl of the Danube."

"Politically, it has an independent city government on the surface. But as you cardinals know, the city is controlled by the Marquis of Hungary. He manipulated the puppet government," Caterina explained.

"Enough, Caterina. We didn't come here to study geopolitical situations," a masculine voice interjected.

The stained-glass windows depicting crusaders wielding swords against evil creatures illuminated a wide room. A beautiful woman with wings was swinging a sword against the largest beast.

They were in the Dark Saint's Room in San Angelo Castle. Scarlet- and purple-robed figures sat at the large, circular table in the center. Minister of Papal State Affairs, Chief Surveyor of Religious Treasures, Minister of Public Affairs, Chaplain of Security, and other important executives of the Vatican's core sat at the table.

From the opposite side of the table, a man with saberlike eyes demanded, "Caterina, what is your point? A few days ago, during their patrol of the east border, my security units were shot at by an unknown, armed group. Did you confirm that it was Istavan's City Military Police who shot at them?" His words were strong and manly. He wore a scarlet cardinal's robe, and he looked like the type of military leader who would stand with his men on the front lines.

He was Duke of Florence, Cardinal Francesco di Medici. An illegitimate child of the previous Pope and half brother of the current Pope, he was an executive in charge of the Department of Inquisition in the Vatican, Secretary of Vatican Papal Doctrine, and Commander of the Vatican Military.

Francesco heaved his broad chest as he howled, "Although it was along the border, my unit was shot at while they were on the Vatican side. This is no good, having Vatican soldiers attacked in their own territory. We should punish the town of Istavan—get rid of the vampires that run it. What is everyone else's opinion?"

"Wait, brother," Caterina softly interrupted, raising her hand. "I did not confirm that the gunfire came from the Istavan City Military Police. I just said that is was a high possibility, that's all."

In contrast to her gruff brother, Caterina was a very calm woman who was in her mid-twenties. Behind her monocle hid a pretty face that expressed both anxiety and boredom, but she stood proudly like a noble. She also wore the scarlet robe of a cardinal—one of the powerful executives that controlled the Vatican.

The Duchess of Milan, Cardinal Caterina Sforza, continued her argument with her razorlike eye twinkling behind her monocle. "In addition to that, Istavan's vampire, the Marquis of Hungary, has allowed and supported the city government from the shadows. If we intrude their city without concrete evidence, the public will not be pleased. We must observe them quietly for a little while longer until we can gather enough evidence to present."

Several members supported her argument. Most of the older cardinals nodded their head in agreement. "Hm, Cardinal Sforza's perspective does make sense."

"We easily could squash Istavan's vampire. But if we move our military without proper justification, the nobles and the common people surely would object," one said.

"Exactly. Times have changed. The common people have forgotten their gratitude and persist in finding our weaknesses," said another.

"The Marquis of Hungary probably wouldn't want to fight the Vatican head on, anyway. As long as he controls the city government from behind the scenes, it's hard for us to lay a finger on him," another cardinal said.

"Do you call yourselves members of the Vatican, backing out of a crusade because you're afraid of public criticism?!" Francesco sharply interjected, pounding his fist on the table. He stood up from his chair and said, "It was wrong in the first place to ignore a city being run by a vampire for so long! Have you forgotten the reason we exist? We are the Vatican. We represent Almighty God!"

A few voices agreed.

"Yes, Cardinal Medici is absolutely right!"

"We represent Almighty God. We shouldn't be afraid!"

Most of the younger cardinals became excited by Francesco's comments, and they started yelling.

Francesco, motivated by the supporters, continued his argument. "Everyone, think about it! We should be deciding how to punish Istavan's vampire! If we eliminate the roots of evil, then the nobles and common people will have nothing to complain about!" Francesco bellowed.

"Well, Cardinal Medici insists on eliminating the roots of evil, but . . ." Caterina smiled sarcastically, but her eyes were cold. "How would you do that? Will you please give us the details?"

"Easy enough," Francesco growled back at his half sister. "We'll deploy military units to Istavan and take over the city. We'll have the units scour the city streets, find the vampires, and burn them at the stake. It is our duty to carry out His will as representative of Almighty God. Do you not agree, Pope?"

The last question was asked to the quiet person sitting between Caterina and Francesco.

"Huh? Uh, take over the ci–city?" a young boy in his early teens stuttered. Unlike his strong half brother and half sister, the boy in the middle didn't seem too bright. He was skinny and frail; had a flat, freckled face; and didn't have a strong presence or aura. But he wore a white robe and cap, indicating that he was indeed the most powerful executive in the Vatican—the Pope.

"S–so, you're suggesting a w–war, my brother? Sister?" the Pope stammered and looked at Caterina. "We're trying to go to war with Istavan?"

"Yes, and worse. It could spread beyond Istavan," Caterina answered. She pointed at the hologram at the center of the table. She tried her best to explain things as simply as possible to her half brother. "Think about the geography, Alec. South of Istavan is the Vatican, to the north and west is the Germanic Kingdom—with a slew of other nobles and commoners—and to the east is the Empire. If we take over the city, how will these neighboring entities react? In order for us to deploy troops, we must have proper justification to keep them quiet."

"I–I–I see. Brother, she is right. We must have proper justification," the Pope reiterated.

"Caterina! Stop filling the Pope's mind with nonsense!" Francesco yelled.

"Eek!" The Pope jerked. The young man almost fainted at the bellowing voice. He tried to hide in his half sister's shadow.

Francesco kicked his chair. "We, as the representatives of God, cannot be weak at a time like this! They are the ones who instigated this conflict. Why do we hesitate when we must punish them?" Francesco demanded.

"We don't have enough *evidence*. Even if the Istavan City Military Police did fire upon your unit, we must investigate their motives. *Why* are they challenging us?" Caterina objected.

"As Minister of Papal State Affairs, that's *your* job, Caterina!" Francesco bellowed.

"I have already begun. But I would like to have some time. As Minister of Papal State Affairs, I cannot condone hasty military operations before conducting a thorough investigation," Caterina defended.

Their eyes blazed. Both of them remained stubborn and firmly stood their ground.

"If you insist, I suppose we can wait." Francesco rubbed his neck and unexpectedly backed off. "I'll wait one week. Do your so-called investigation during that time."

"Thank you very much," Caterina replied.

"But—" Francesco changed the tone of his voice. He looked down at Caterina and continued, "If your investigation doesn't produce results, then we will conduct a forceful investigation of Istavan and deploy the military! Do you have any objections to that?"

†

Caterina retreated to her office, muttering, "Waiting one week; yeah, right—so that time can be used to prepare his troops?! He's such a sly fox, isn't he?"

She wasn't strongly against military deployment. She knew at times there was a need to have the Vatican enforce its authority over those that opposed them. But the problem was finding the proper justification to do so. She needed to find evidence to prove Istavan's anti-Vatican activities to the public.

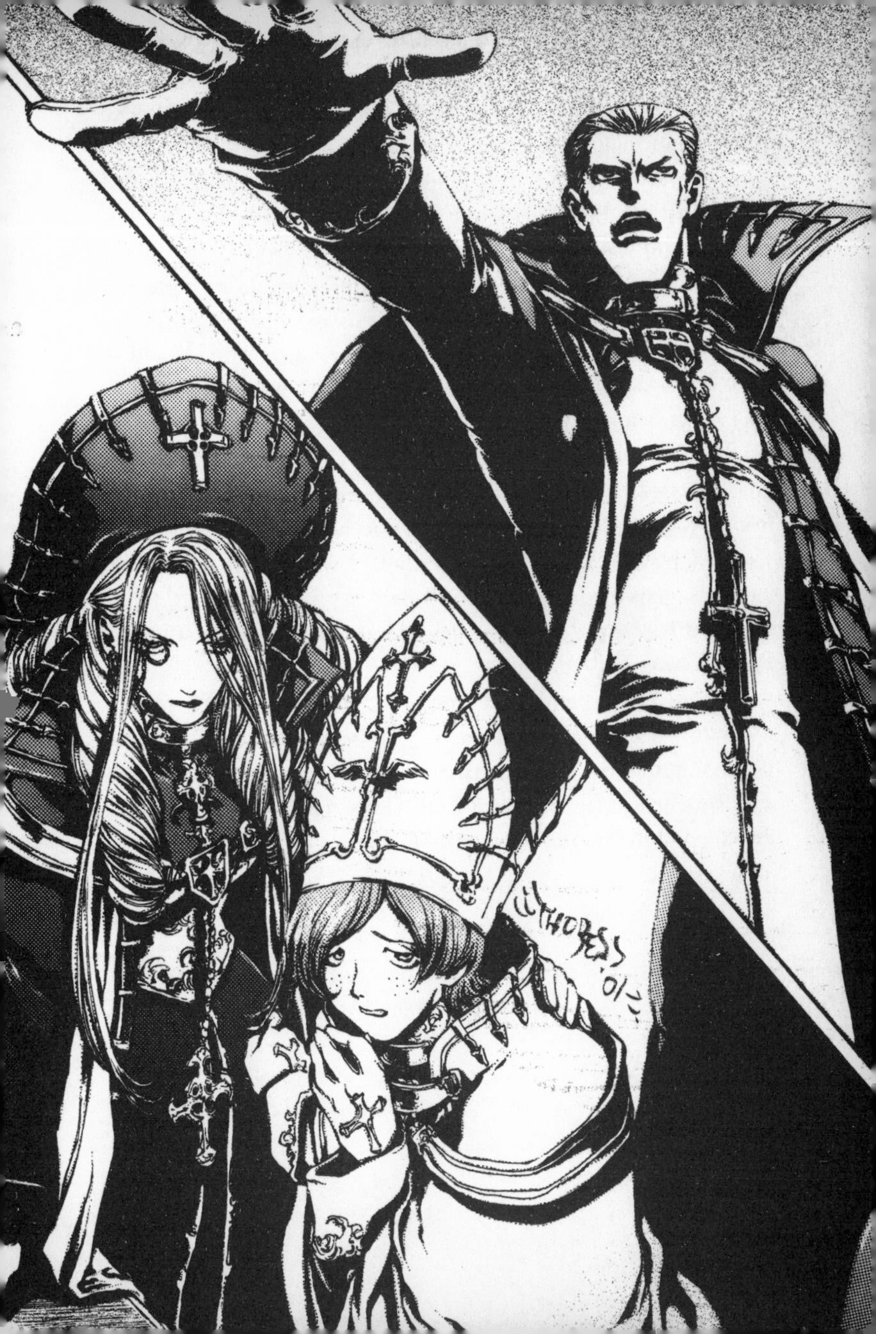
THORES '01

It had been a thousand years since the Armageddon. The Vatican lost public support, while the nobles and commoners gained power by the day. Francesco and his young cardinal supporters still believed in the illusion of a strong Vatican, but the situation was more complex than that. As soon as the Vatican invaded Istavan, the nobles and commoners would criticize the Vatican more harshly. And she wished to avoid upsetting the only non-human nation, the Empire.

In order to avoid these possible negative effects, she had to find convincing justification.

Caterina clasped her hands, deep in thought. Moments later, she looked up and called out, "Are you there, Sister Kate?"

"Yes, Your Eminence," replied the hologram of a nun. She had droopy eyes, but she seemed kind. "I was just about to . . . Is this an urgent matter, Your Eminence?"

"What is the status of *Iron Maiden II?* Is it operational?" Caterina asked.

"Yes. We can embark at any time," replied Kate.

"Outstanding. Please go to Istavan immediately," Caterina ordered. Kate bowed as Caterina continued, "I wish to give a new supplemental order to Crusnik and Gunslinger, who are currently conducting infiltration operations. There is something I want them to investigate."

BANQUE+ IN +HE DARK

For they will come to slay thee; yea,
in the night will they come to slay thee.
—*Nehemiah 6:10*

I

The night was quiet, dark, and gray. The streets, seen through the car window, were similar to those of a large city. The trees were capped with a soft layer of cottony snow, and the stone tiles were illuminated softly by the glow of the street lamps. Though it wasn't as beautiful as Rome, it was almost as beautiful as large cities like Londinium and Vienna.

But upon closer observation, the ruins of this city could not be ignored.

Half of the street lamps were broken; several stone tiles were peeling and cracked; and though it was still early in the evening, almost no one walked the streets. There were police stations on nearly every street corner, and armed military police were on patrol.

Poverty and ruin—this town was no longer the glamorous Pearl of the Danube it used to be.

"Wow, this town is desolate. It's like the whole place is a slum," Abel remarked.

"The anti-government terrorist group, the Partisans, caused all this," the giant responded bitterly, as Abel pressed his nose to the window to ogle the town. Chuckling as if to make fun of Abel's ignorance, Radcon continued, "The terrorists have destroyed all sorts of public structures around town. They steal food meant to be distributed to the people, and they randomly destroy gas and water pipes. The town has gone to hell because of that. And they've murdered several people."

"They're really bad, aren't they?" Abel sighed. The two moons peeked through the clouds and barely lit up the city. Yet some of the street lamps remained unlit.

"Um, so City Military Police? Colonel, your unit also acts as the police, right? Can't you arrest those bad people?" Abel asked.

"Of course. But there are still a lot of them hiding in the woodwork. No matter how many we crush, they keep coming out like cockroaches," Radcon replied.

"That's a tough job indeed . . . What's that?" Abel exclaimed.

At the southern end of the main street—and the edge of the Danube River—there was a large, shining object, illuminating the car shadows.

"Steel bridge. The only bridge connecting Buda to Pest," Radcon replied.

The large bridge was covered with lights. Each of the bridge's legs was decorated with a sculpture that was individually illuminated, making the string of lights look like a chain. The lights reflected off the water's surface—the awesome sight was enough to make one forget the chill of winter.

"Stop!" a guard ordered, and the car came to a screeching halt right before entering the bridge. Machine guns and flashlights poked out of the guardhouse, and an armed guard appeared.

"It's Radcon. I'm taking a guest to the Valley of Blood," Radcon announced.

"We received notification, sir. Have a good evening, Colonel!" The guard saluted. The sergeant major signaled to the guardhouse, and the roadblocks collapsed to the ground with a squealing sound. The car drove onto the bridge.

"That's a lot of security," remarked Abel as he looked back at the guard. The bridge was guarded like a fort. And next to the guardhouse was an armored vehicle.

"Wasn't that a new type of Germanic armored car? Aren't those expensive?" Abel asked.

"No, not really. I heard they cost only five hundred thousand dinars," Radcon answered.

"Five hundred thousand dinars?!" Abel screeched. *With that kind of money, one could rebuild Saint Mathias Church and still get a lot of change back.*

"That's a bazillion times more than my pay. But anyway . . ." Abel muttered. "Er, maybe you should use that money to rebuild the city and calm the Partisans a bit?"

Radcon snorted.

The car kept climbing a sharp incline. Instead of street lamps, searchlights illuminated the mountainous roads and made it seem as bright as day.

"So this is the Valley of Blood. Where is Lord Gyula's estate?" Abel asked.

"What the hell?" Radcon looked at Abel. "The area on this side of the bridge is Lord Gyula's land. You're already on his estate."

"Huh? S-so, this mountain, too?" Abel gasped.

"Not only this mountain; the whole Buda province is his. Okay, we're here," Radcon said.

"Here! What is that?" Abel asked, nodding to the huge, white monument atop the mountain. It was an elegant baroque palace.

The vast estate was sprawling with neatly trimmed greenery. There were several fountains and summer homes in the front yard; each seemed to come straight from a fairy tale. Compared to the rustic town of Buda, the mansion in Pest was luxurious.

After getting out of the car at the front entrance loop, Abel sighed in amazement.

"I brought Father Abel Nightroad. Please inform Lord Gyula," Radcon announced.

"We have been waiting for you. Please come this way, Father Nightroad," a mechanical maid responded at the entrance. The face underneath her blue hair was pretty, but she didn't seem alive. This was another salvaged lost technology before the Armageddon—a robot, or a non-AI servant.

Only high-ranking priests or extravagantly rich nobles could afford this expensive toy. The Kadar clan must be a really wealthy and influential family, considering that he controls City Military Police and lives in a palace, Abel thought. *What a big difference between here and the other side of the bridge.*

"Okay. See you later, Father," Radcon said as Abel stepped into the palace. Abel noticed that Radcon's face was twitching, filled with both ridicule and pity. "I'm sure you have a lot of things left undone, but I'll take care of things from here. Especially that novice. She's a fighter, all right, but a real beauty. I'll take good care of her in your place, okay?"

"Thank you for your kind consideration, but I'll return tomorrow." Abel smiled back. "It's pretty late already. Once I finish eating dinner, I'll go home immediately," Abel announced.

"Go home immediately? Did you hear that?!" Radcon pounded the car's roof and laughed. The driver laughed, too, but he seemed nervous.

"Sorry, but Lord Gyula takes care of his guests. He won't let you go that easily. You can try all you want, though, I'm sure." Radcon laughed. He got in the car and took off in a hurry.

Abel raised his collar and saw the red taillights disappear into the darkness.

The robot stated, "This way, Father Nightroad."

Abel turned around and followed the robot, his foot almost sinking into the soft carpet. The main doors shut behind him.

None of the candles were lit on the chandelier. Only the moonlight shone onto the central courtyard, which was vast enough to fit a small house. Compared with Abel's guest room, this was at least fifty times larger. At the far end were double glass doors, with the terrace behind them. On the right was a large staircase; and above, spreading both ways, staircases led to the library and the chess room. On the left . . .

"Wow, she's beautiful," Abel commented, indicating the woman depicted in the framed painting on the wall. She was a young lady with long, wavy black hair. She wore a dress that opened at her neckline. *It seems to be a fairly old painting, but I wonder who she is?* Abel pondered.

"That's my wife. She passed away a long time ago," replied Gyula.

Abel turned around to see a young nobleman at the top of the staircase. He wore a dark suit with a dark blue sash and tie, which contrasted well.

His presence was typical of an elegant nobleman; he illuminated everything around him. He was proud and decorous, walking gracefully down the stairs and bowing to Abel. "I apologize for the sudden nature of your visit, Father Nightroad. I'm sure you were surprised to receive my invitation."

"N-no, not at all! Thank you for inviting me!" Abel replied.

"Excuse me. Please have a seat. I would like to propose a toast for our meeting." Gyula smiled while he snapped his fingers. A butler holding a large metallic candlestick entered the room. Several servants pushing metal carts trailed behind him. All of them were as silent and expressionless as the robot at the front entrance.

"You have a lot of robots," Abel remarked.

"I don't like humans," Gyula replied. "The robots take care of all my needs here. I like them because they're quiet."

Gyula took a white goblet from the maid standing next to him. He filled it with a red drink and savored it. "Ah, this tastes wonderful. Please pour some for the guest."

The red wine was thick and ripe. The sweetness and bitterness balanced well.

"Oh, this is really good! Very tasty! What wine is this?" Abel asked.

"Bull's Blood. My winery makes it. It has high marks. We use great fertilizer," Gyula answered.

"What sort of fertilizer do you use?" Abel asked as he finished off a second glass of wine.

Gyula's gray eyes playfully peered at Abel as he chuckled. "Blood. A lot of human blood is in it."

Abel was shocked and almost spit out the wine. He couldn't swallow it anymore, so the wine just sloshed inside his mouth.

"Just kidding, Father. Don't worry: It's not human blood. I just put a drop or two of butchered cow's blood," Gyula laughed.

"Oh, you had me for a moment." Abel swallowed and groaned. His eyes filled with tears. "You scared me, Lord Gyula. I was about to spit it out."

"I'm so sorry. I didn't think you'd be that surprised." Gyula chuckled in the darkness. He continued to sip his drink; then he remarked, "But how peculiar."

"What?" Abel asked.

"Your reaction just now. Duck blood sauce, blood sausage— there are many dishes that use blood. Why were you so alarmed at fertilizer using blood?" Gyula inquired.

"Well, those dishes are made from animal blood, not human," Abel replied.

"I see. Wasn't there a passage in the Bible stating 'Those who eat blood will be destroyed'? I suppose animal blood is okay, though," Gyula remarked. He sipped more wine, but the way he stared into Abel's eyes made the priest queasy and nervous.

Abel finally gathered his strength and replied, "By the way, Lord Gyula, may I ask you a question?"

"Sure," he stated.

"On the way here, I saw Pest province. I was shocked at the state of ruin there. You're the only one living extravagantly. Don't you want to help out the other townspeople somehow?" Abel asked.

"The town residents?" Gyula chuckled as if he heard a sick joke. His gray eyes filled with malice. "Why do I have to please the townspeople? They're just herd animals—they should be happy they're kept alive."

"Herd animals? That's a little rude to call fellow humans that," Abel commented.

"Fellow humans? Fellow *humans?!*" Gyula retorted, his voice full of darkness.

The priest looked up to see shining wolflike eyes.

"Don't put me in the same category as them, Father," Gyula exclaimed. "Don't think I'm the same as those lowly creatures!"

"S-sorry . . ." Abel apologized and shook his head. He felt as if the whole house were pressing down on him.

"Pardon me. I got a bit excited." Gyula coughed and calmed down. He looked up to the painting on the wall and remarked, "My wife said the same thing you did. 'They're fellow humans, like you.' My wife treated the townspeople well. On nights like this, she'd pass out candy and medicine to them, even though I told her to stop doing so."

Gyula looked up to his wife's painting, reminiscing about the past. But when he looked at Abel, his eyes held an evil look again. "One summer, a plague hit the town. Many of the townspeople fell ill. My wife was worried about them and passed out medicine. But she never returned. She was killed." Gyula continued.

"Killed?" Abel asked.

"Yes—killed by those townspeople she helped!" Gyula huffed, tipping his goblet to one side. His lips were stained red.

Abel noticed the decanter had a different liquid than his—it was a murky red color, unlike his own wine.

"They're animals, filthy animals. And we need to protect our own kind, no matter what it takes," Gyula affirmed. He rang a bell and the servants brought trays of food and laid them on the table in front of Abel. One tray had a large cover on it.

"Um, Lord Gyula, I think . . ." Abel spoke as he lifted the tray cover. "I'm very sorry for your wife's predicament. But I don't think you should hate all townspeople . . . huh?" Abel gulped. He blinked at the round object on the tray—a hairy, round object . . .

It was a bloody human head.

"Waaaaah!" Abel shrieked and crawled backward.

"Oh, you don't like that?" Gyula chuckled Abel's retreat. "He's the Partisan that attacked me at the train station. A putrid Terran trying to go up against Methuselah."

Abel's face froze. "Terran?! Methuselah?!" Those were terms vampires used for humans and vampires, respectively.

And the nobleman referred to the townspeople as "herd animals." He was not making fun of them; rather, he accurately described them from a vampire's perspective.

"L-Lord Gyula, a-are you a va-va-va . . ." Abel stuttered. "Vampire?!"

"I don't like that term." Gyula's voice came from behind Abel. When Abel turned around to look, the young nobleman was no longer sitting at the table but standing right behind him.

"Our kind feeds on the blood of humans. To call us monsters because of that is rude. But I suppose it's okay for now," Gyula commented.

Abel let out a shriek.

Gyula had grabbed his shoulders. His mouth, reeking of blood, neared the priest's neck.

Gyula continued, "I hate priests. They preach love but kill us in the name of peace. They kill our women and children, too, because we're different. The person who killed my wife was a Vatican agent like yourself, Father Nightroad."

He tensed his grip on the priest. Fangs poked out of Gyula's mouth.

"Eek!" Abel couldn't resist.

Gyula's powerful arms pulled the priest close to him; he placed his lips on the priest's neck. His ivory fangs sank into Abel's white skin. But as he was about to pierce skin, the center court reverberated.

"What?!" Gyula exclaimed. All the windowpanes shattered, glass showering onto the floor like snow. One of the robots that stood by at the side of the room was blown to smithereens.

Gyula pulled away from Abel's neck to look around the room. He saw a large ball of fire at one end of his palace.

"Is that the ammunition storage?!" Gyula yelled. *Was it an accident? But sparks flew from the flames! What is that?* Gyula walked toward the window.

The main entrance doors stood wide open, with a group of masked men on the other side of the door.

Gyula yelled at the group pointing guns at him. "Partisans!"

"Fire!" a voice ordered, and the men fired their weapons in unison. Multiple shots hit the robot next to Gyula, and it exploded. The small archer in the center of the group ordered, "Gyula! Forget the pawns and go for Gyula!"

"Are you Star?" Gyula asked.

The archer pulled the trigger, trying to shoot an arrow into the vampire's heart.

"Don't underestimate me, Terran!" Gyula said as he dodged the arrow.

Gyula entered haste mode by stimulating his body's nervous system into overdrive; during that brief period, he could move twenty times faster. All vampires had these gifted powers.

None of the rounds hit the nobleman, but they shattered the sculpture behind him into a pile of crumbs.

He caught a thick arrow with his hand.

"Here, have it back!" Gyula threw the arrow toward one of the Partisans, piercing the man's chest.

The arrow was tipped with silver nitrate, and when it touched flesh, it created a burning odor. The impaled man dropped to the ground, convulsing.

"Ra-Rayosh!" Star tried to go the fallen man.

But a skinny, drab-eyed youth holding a machine pistol stopped his leader. As he sprayed shots on full auto, he yelled, "Don't go, Star! He's no good. Leave him! Hurry and save the priest!"

"B-but, Dietrich—" Star said.

"Hurry!" the man insisted.

The figure named Star stood there for a moment, biting its lower lip before finally deciding to go for it and pulling down a gas mask.

Star yelled, "Everyone, cover me!" before rapidly running into the room where the vampire was. Arrows continued to spray along the way, springing toward Gyula's heart.

"Star, did you come here to get killed?" Gyula snapped the thick arrow with his fingers. Twenty Terran were no match for one Methuselah.

But the Methuselah didn't know that the arrow he broke was loaded with gunpowder—it exploded.

"What?!" Gyula was surprised, but the injuries didn't stop him. Getting a few fingers blown off wasn't too damaging for a Methuselah. The fingers would grow back overnight. Despite the small scale of the explosion, however, the amount of white smoke that it produced was enough to cover the entire room.

"Smoke bomb!" Gyula exclaimed.

Even a Methuselah couldn't evade this. It was a tear gas bomb, which made a screen of smoke that irritated the eyes and nose. A Methuselah's super sensitive sense of smell always overreacted to the stinging gas.

"Dammit! What a dirty trick, Star!" Gyula scoffed. He saw a small figure run toward the tall, slinky man, dragging him toward the terrace.

"Over here, Father Nightroad! Hurry!" said Star.

Coughing, Abel managed to say, "Wh-what . . . ? Whoa!" Abel was kicked out the window, and Star followed right behind him. The explosion of the ammunition storage brightened the center court.

"Over here!" Someone waved a lantern from the dry well.

Star pulled Abel to his feet and asked, "Can you make it over there, Father Nightroad?"

"Uh, I suppose. By the way, Esther, why are you doing this?" Abel asked.

Star stayed silent for a moment, and then she pulled off her gas mask. Her neatly tucked auburn hair fanned outward.

The girl with blue eyes asked Abel, "When did you notice, Father?"

"When I talked about the gunfight at the train station, you mentioned that I was 'lucky to escape without injuries.' How did you know I wasn't hurt?" Abel pointed out.

"I guess I talk too much." Esther scooped her red hair away from her cheek.

They could make out the faint voices of City Military Police that were gathering in the area.

A large man at the dry well hollered, "Hey, hurry! The others already have retreated!" The smoke behind him was starting to clear. It was wise to leave soon.

"We will retreat to our hideout for now. Father, please follow me closely!" Esther ordered.

II

Under the swinging ceiling lamp, men and women in traditional attire were engaged in a vigorous regional dance. The men's faces were red from whistling and clapping to the simple sounds of the accordion and hurdy-gurdy. While they happily joked and laughed, they passed around brandy and wine from barrels. Considering that this place was underneath a winery, there was plenty of good food and wine to go around.

Besides that, there were copy machines piled with pamphlets, strange machinery lined up, and a submachine gun leaned against a press.

"Well, I thought Partisans had a hideout in the mountains or something. I didn't expect it to be smack in the middle of town," Abel remarked.

"It's harder to find us within the city. After all, they say, 'hide a tree in a forest.' Here you go, Father." Esther handed him a warm drink in a cup.

Abel carefully took the hot milk as he sat next to the girl. "Thank you. This is delicious, Esther," Abel said.

"I made this in a hurry because you said you didn't want alcohol." Esther smiled at Abel, who had a white ring around his mouth. Her eyes drooped slightly and she looked younger than her actual age of seventeen. No one would suspect she was Star, the leader of the local criminal terrorist organization. Abel still couldn't believe that this pleasant little girl had saved him from that fiasco hours before.

"What's wrong, Father?" Esther curiously peered into Abel's face with her lapis lazuli eyes.

"Huh?!" Abel broke his train of thought.

"Is there something on my face?" Esther asked.

"Uh, nothing, really." Abel coughed. He tried to change the subject. "Er, Sister Esther. Are you really the leader of the Partisans, Istavan's human liberation group? You actually run this organization and tell these people to conduct anti-government activities?" Abel asked.

"Well, yes, pretty much. But I wouldn't say I run the organization." Esther tilted her head, trying to find the right words. "I just pull these people together. As far as pay and funding goes, the townspeople donate the money, and Ignatz, the bar owner, takes care of us. But the mastermind of the operations is Dietrich. Dietrich, can you come here?"

A young man broke away from a lively conversation and headed toward the girl. "What is it, Esther? Hi, Father Nightroad," he said as sat down on the other side of Esther. He shook Abel's hand. "I'm Dietrich von Lohengrin. Nice to meet you."

"Nice to meet you too." Abel shook his hand.

Dietrich was a handsome young man; and judging from his name, he probably was a student from the Germanic Kingdom. His thin face almost could be described as pretty.

Abel tried to suck in his cheeks to mimic Dietrich's handsome features.

Esther gave him a blanket and asked, "Are you cold, Father?"

"So, did you explain everything to the priest, Esther?" Dietrich asked.

"I was just about to. As you probably know by now, vampires control this town. The ringleader is the Marquis of Hungary and his clan," Esther replied, whispering the word "vampire" out of fear. "On the surface, Istavan seems to be a free city; but in reality, they've controlled it for several hundred years. They own the factories, banks, farms, and everything else of value. And the city council is just for show. City Military Police obviously are their pawns."

Dietrich added in a serious tone, "And the townspeople are their food."

"You saw the town, right, Father? Everyone has been pushed to their limits. The marquis raised taxes to fund his military equipment. Those who cannot pay the taxes are arrested by the police and locked up. No one ever comes back," Esther continued.

Abel interrupted, "But wait. Aren't you guys responsible for the destruction of the town, too? I heard that your people destroy public property, steal food, and kill others."

"The only places we attack are City Military Police facilities!" Esther retorted. "When we rescue people from prison, we take back the food the police stole from us. I admit, we did fight City Military Police, and we took some lives. But if we don't do that . . ." Esther choked on her words.

"Esther . . ." Dietrich wrapped his arm around Esther. He glared at the priest and asked, "Father, you call us murderers, but what else can we do? Just stand by and wait to be eaten by them? Even the church has forsaken us. The only option is to dirty our hands with blood."

"The church has forsaken this town? Can't the bishop do anything to help? If there are so many vampire activities in this city, then she should report it to Rome and ask for a crusade," Abel suggested.

"Father, you don't get it, do you?" Dietrich shook his head in disappointment. "Why do you think the vampires were able to run this town for centuries? Are you unaware of what lies to the east of the Carpathian Mountains?"

"You mean the Empire." Abel lowered his head in shame.

The Empire, officially called the New Human Empire, was a large country located east of Istavan. The territory spanned from the east of the Carpathian Mountains to the coast of the Black Sea, which was roughly the eastern half of the inhabitable lands. If Methuselah utilized their powers and effectively recovered the lost technology, then they could be as strong as the Vatican, if not stronger.

Though the country was vast, much remained unknown. The identity of the imperial leader and the motives of the noble clans there were still a mystery because it was the only nation established by non-humans. All the citizens, including the imperial family and clans, were vampires.

"To the west of this town is the Vatican, and to the east is the Empire. We lie between the humans and vampires. If the Vatican invades this place, another Armageddon might occur. That's why Rome is extremely careful when dealing with this town. Actually, it's better to say that Rome has abandoned the people here," Dietrich explained.

"But regardless of whether the Vatican has abandoned us, these people will live and die here. The only option for them is to fight for their loved ones," Esther said with conviction.

Abel thought the loyalty sparkling in her blue eyes was the reason she could bring together the townspeople.

Esther continued, "It's true that we just caused a ruckus on his estate. But even that is a large victory for us. The other townspeople will know that the vampires aren't invincible."

"But it's too bad we couldn't destroy the Star of Sorrow. We were almost there," Dietrich added.

"The Star of what?" Abel asked.

"The Star of Sorrow—it's the ultimate weapon of the Marquis of Hungary," Dietrich patiently answered. "According to legend, it was one of the lost technologies from before Armageddon—or rather, one of the weapons that brought about Armageddon."

"Brought about . . . ? What type of weapon is it? Is it a large cannon or something?" Abel inquired.

"We don't know. According to rumors, it supposedly can draw in a curtain of fire from the sky . . . or cause large earthquakes or something. But only the marquis can operate this weapon," Dietrich answered.

"Well, that's quite scary. Wait. If the Marquis of Hungary has such a weapon, then why doesn't he just flick the switch and obliterate the Vatican in Rome?" Abel asked.

"The large weapon seems to have been damaged a long time ago. But there are rumors that he was able to repair it recently. Our intelligence sources also reveal large amounts of expensive machinery were purchased by the marquis," Dietrich replied.

Esther coughed and interrupted Dietrich's lecture. "Now that you know all this, we need a commitment from you, Father." She stared at the overwhelmed Abel and recommended, "As long as you're in town, you must avoid the marquis, especially after the incident tonight. For your sake, I suggest you stick with us, okay?"

"Well, after all that happened tonight, I can't go back to the church. I guess I need to follow you for life," Abel lamented.

"Eh?! Uh, well, I didn't ask for a lifelong commitment. . . ." Esther sputtered.

"Lord, my life is a dead end . . . ! Ah, I'm out of milk. May I have another cup?" Abel sniffed.

"Huh? Sure. Go upstairs to the kitchen." Esther pointed. She watched Abel sob as he went upstairs.

Dietrich whispered, "Is that priest okay? He might slow us down."

She thought about it. "Well, we can't just let him out on the streets, either. He doesn't seem too useful, but I'll watch him, so don't worry."

Dietrich wanted to continue, but he noticed Esther's determined look, so he stopped. He chuckled and shrugged his shoulders. "Well, I do like your big, forgiving heart."

✝

"Why am I so unlucky?" the priest lamented with a sigh as he warmed a pot of milk on the kitchen stove upstairs. The sun was about to rise, causing the sky to turn blue. It was a long night. It felt like forty or fifty hours had passed.

"I thought I'd be able to relax in the countryside, but the first day here was so hectic. I don't have enough lives to last here. Oh Lord, it seems that my life is so troubled," Abel prayed.

"Aren't you always in trouble, Father Abel?" a familiar woman's soft voice said merrily. There was no one else in the kitchen. But Abel didn't seem surprised as he clicked on his ear cuffs.

"Good evening, Sister Kate. Err, I mean, good morning. When did you get here?" Abel asked.

"I arrived just now. Gunslinger finished reporting to me moments ago. I heard that the City Military Police are planning to execute a large-scale military operation soon. Also, there are several armored vehicles that moved out of the city. Aren't those tanks?" Kate said.

Abel looked out the barred window, but he could see only a row of shacks along the streets below. *Where's she seeing these activities?*

"Well, this is happening right after that little commotion. I suppose it's natural for the police to react. Gunslinger will probably be occupied for a while, poor man," Kate said with a sigh.

"Sister Kate, what did Gunslinger report? What is the target?" Abel asked.

"I'm not sure. So far, City Military Police decided to enhance surveillance of the church, though," Kate responded.

There was only one church in Istavan.

"So, are they finally going to put pressure on the church?" Abel asked.

"Cardinal Caterina hopes to bring all the clergy back to Rome. But if Rome makes such a movement, then it might agitate them unnecessarily," Kate continued.

"If so, then we need to find a way to have the clergy escape covertly. That's hard," Abel remarked.

"We need to alert them so they can make preparations, though," Kate added.

Abel was deep in thought as he stirred the bubbling pot. Finally, he decided. "That's the only way. I'll ask the Partisans to help them out. As Gunslinger said, the Partisans are a very talented group."

"Father Abel, about the Partisans . . ." Kate muttered. "There is one problem: Right before the attack, City Military Police transported most of the ammunition out of the armory warehouse. It's too peculiar to be a coincidence."

"Someone is leaking information about the Partisans?" Abel deduced.

"Apparently. Please watch your back. I'll contact you again. I will stand by here."

"Roger. Stay alert, Iron Maiden." Abel tapped his ear cuffs, cutting off the transmission. He continued to stir the bubbling pot while he contemplated things. He needed to discuss this with Esther.

III

Andrassy Avenue—known as the Heroes' Avenue, it is the main street running from east to west of Pest. This area was the economic center of Istavan more than a thousand years ago, long before the Armageddon, when it was the capital of the ruling kingdom. Even though the city was in ruins, merchant shops and fancy street lamps were left over from bustling times. On Sundays, people still flocked to the flea markets, secondhand clothing stores, and black market food sellers. No matter how desolate the place was, people would still gather as long as things flowed there.

"So this is the black market. Won't City Military Police come if you do this openly?" Abel whispered.

"If they get bribed, no. Actually, there are some City Military Policeman selling here, too, like at that secondhand clothing shop. That store is selling stolen military goods," Dietrich replied.

Many people turned to notice a tall young man, who had light brown hair and wore a priest's robe.

"Why are we walking the main street just to go to church, Dietrich?" the nun with glasses asked. "Maybe we should go through the back alleys."

"The alleys are full of City Military Police. And there are fewer people there, so we'd stick out more," Dietrich replied.

"That's true. I'd stick out, all right." The extremely tall nun tucked silvery blond bangs behind a veil. Then, six-foot tall Abel shook his head as he complained to the smaller nun next to him, "I want to go back to Rome. Why am I wearing this outfit, anyway . . . ?"

"Well, Father Ni—I mean, Sister Avelina—City Military Police know your face. And it would be strange for a commoner to enter the church at this time of day," Esther responded seriously as she tried to hold back her laughter.

"And you look nice in that outfit," Esther said with a chuckle.

"Wh-why are you chuckling?!" Abel spouted.

"Shh! Quiet!" Dietrich hissed.

A squad of military police, rifles slung over their shoulders, approached from a distance.

The three conspirators quickly looked down, and the police passed by them without noticing anything. After the police left, the trio turned the corner.

"Be more careful, Sister Avelina," Esther warned.

Abel tried to reply, but Dietrich cut him off, saying, "There's the church."

They hurried toward the building, careful to ensure that the police did not notice them.

"Bishop!" Esther cried out.

Bishop Vitez stopped raking the yard to look up. Her face brightened when she saw Esther approaching her. "Esther, where have you been? We have been looking for you since you disappeared last night. We were so worried about you."

Vitez hugged Esther warmly, but then she noticed a strange figure standing there. "Is that you, Father Nightroad?"

"Uh, yes. Good afternoon." Abel nodded.

Bishop Vitez sensed that something was wrong when she looked at Abel's peculiar outfit, so she kept Esther in her arms as she stepped back and said, "Please come inside. Tell me what happened."

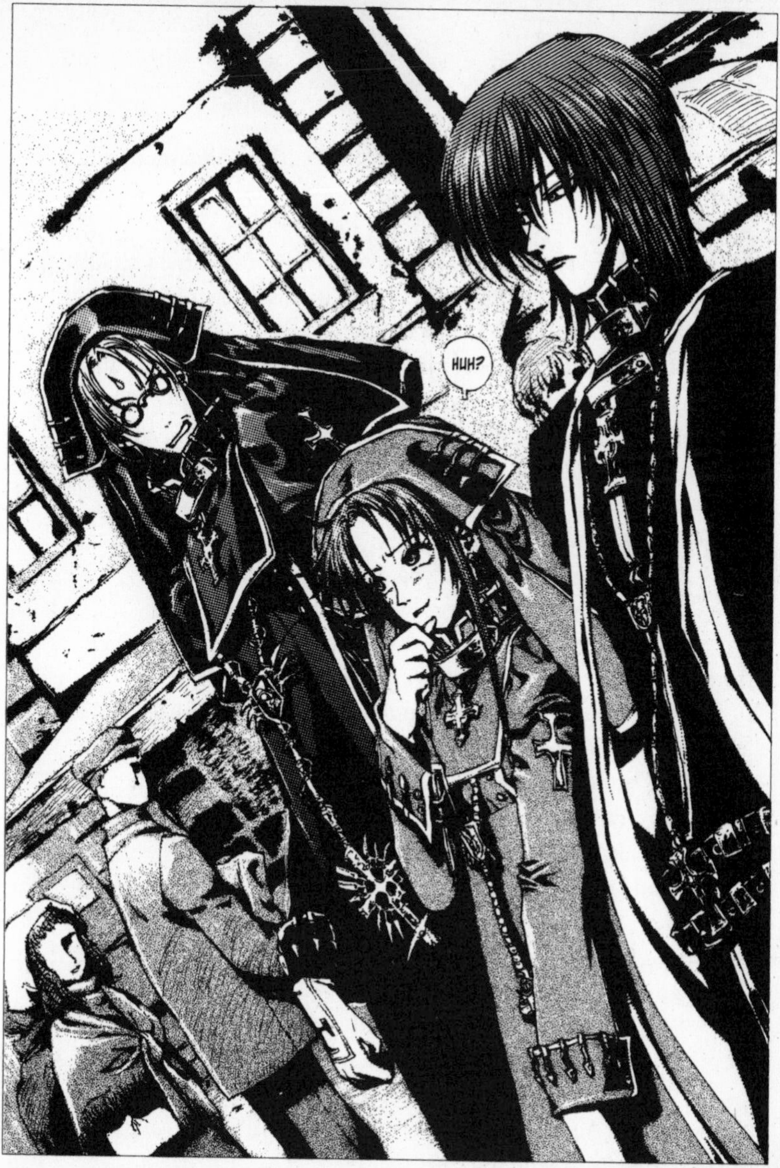
HUH?

✝

Vitez stayed calm as she listened to Esther's confession and warning. She sipped her tea and asked, "So, Esther, what do you want us to do?"

"Please have the clergy leave town. The marquis tried to kill Father Nightroad. According to him, the marquis despises clergymen, so he will try to destroy this church next."

"I see. But the vampires have left us alone for so long. Why are they after us now?" Vitez asked.

"I don't know. But maybe the situation has changed. This place is no longer safe," Esther warned. "Tomorrow morning, a merchant caravan will leave for Vienna, so please ride with them, Bishop. I've already coordinated with the caravan chief."

"All right But what will you do?" Vitez inquired.

"Father Nightroad will go with you," Esther replied.

"Stop changing the subject. I am asking about you, Esther," Vitez calmly stated. "You *are* leaving town with us, right?"

"I am staying here because everyone else will. I can't just leave them behind," Esther said with conviction, though her voice trembled a bit. The bishop, having known Esther for seventeen years and raised her as if she were a daughter, knew Esther couldn't be convinced otherwise.

"I understand. I will do as you ask. But please promise me one thing," Vitez placed her hand on Esther's veiled head and stared into Esther's eyes. "Please don't overdo it. After all this is over, please promise that you will come see me?"

"Yes, Bishop." Esther nodded and made the sign of the cross. "I promise."

"Good. I suppose we need to pack tonight." Vitez smiled. She turned to Abel and said, "Well, Sister Avelina."

"Please, that's enough," Abel pleaded.

"Okay, Father Nightroad. You are coming with us, right?" Vitez asked.

"Well, I would love to leave town with all of you, but . . ." Abel shrugged. "The Partisans saved my life, so I owe them. I will stay behind."

"No, Father!" Esther exclaimed. She hadn't expected him to say that. "It's too dangerous! Please go with the bishop."

Abel calmly replied, "Well, you and Dietrich risked your lives to save me. I owe you. I don't like owing people for long."

"But, Father," Esther muttered as she glanced at Dietrich, waiting for him to help convince the priest.

Suddenly, there was a violent knock at the door. "Bishop! Bishop! Oh my God!"

Before Vitez could stand up, a balding, middle-aged monk barged into the room.

"What's the matter, Brother Vela?" Vitez asked.

"Ci-City Military Police are here!" the monk stammered.

Before the monk could finish his warning, a commotion arose from the other end of the hallway. Military boots stomped on the floor, and there was the sound of breaking glass. Next, there were screams. Finally, a muffled groan was heard—apparently, one of the monks was beaten for trying to stop the advancement.

"We are looking for the terrorist Abel Nightroad, who attacked the Valley of Blood. He is a priest in this church," a cold, emotionless voice called out. "We received information that this church is protecting the priest. We will begin the search now. All clergymen are requested to cooperate. If you do not cooperate, you will be punished for obstructing justice."

"The police!" Esther peeped through the keyhole and exclaimed. What bad timing. Navy-uniformed men were spread out. Foremost was the expressionless young officer she had seen previously at the train station, Major Tres Iqus. "How could they know already?"

"Esther, this way!" Vitez grabbed Esther's hand and swiftly walked to the bookshelf. At the end of the shelf was a thick, old, leather book. She pushed in the book, and the shelf slid to the side with a rumbling noise. Behind the bookshelf was a shoulder-width tunnel that led to a downward stairway.

"The previous bishop made this—now go!" Vitez ordered.

"But what about you, Bishop?!" Esther cried out as Vitez pushed her forward.

"I can't leave everyone behind. Like you, Esther. I cannot leave my clergy behind, so I will stay," Vitez said.

"Then I'll stay, too!" Esther said.

"No!" Vitez sharply responded. "You have a mission to accomplish. Father Nightroad, please take care of her."

Abel wanted to say something, but Vitez's scared but graceful stare silenced him. He silently pushed Esther forward.

"Bishop . . ." Esther said.

As the opening started to close, Esther turned around to Vitez, whom she considered her only family, and promised, "I will come back for you!"

They went down the dark stairway. Dietrich led the way, with only a small lighter illuminating the area. Esther slipped several times, but the tall priest held her up.

"Go, Esther. Oh Lord, please watch over my daughter," Vitez grasped her rosary as she saw the three figures descend the stairs. She eventually pulled the book back to its original position. Right as the shelf returned to its place, someone kicked open the door.

Vitez sharply warned, "Stand down! This is the house of God!"

"Bishop Vitez, we are conducting peacekeeping operations. We are not concerned about the official purpose of this facility," the young officer leading the group responded. He was not tall, but his dark blue uniform was impeccable. "I am Major Tres Iqus of Special Company, First Regiment. Currently, we are searching for Father Abel Nightroad, who is residing in this church. He faces charges of terrorism in the Buda district. Do you know where he is?"

"No. Even if I did, I would not tell you," Vitez replied.

"There have been reports from citizens that Father Nightroad came to this church today. If you are indeed hiding him from us, then you and the rest of your clergy will suffer the consequences," Tres warned.

"Well, I don't know where he is," Vitez responded.

Tres' hands flashed out and snapped up two large handguns. "I'll ask again," the small officer said, pointing at the bishop's forehead two Jerico M13 "Dies Irae"—the largest combat handguns in the world. "So, will you tell me where the suspect is located?"

"No," the bishop replied.

"Understood." Tres responded with a large crack of gunfire.

Tres fired both guns simultaneously, and the two thirteen-millimeter rounds split the bookcase behind the bishop in half, exposing the hidden stairway.

"Begin pursuit." Tres motioned with his chin, ignoring the bishop, whose eyes were closed. "Try to capture them alive. If they resist, though, you may fire."

"What about her, Major?" A soldier pointed his rifle toward Vitez. "If we arrest her for obstructing justice, Colonel Radcon surely will be pleased," the soldier suggested.

"Negative. That's unnecessary." Tres pointed his smoking gun at the soldier's forehead. The emotionless officer continued, "Our mission is to capture Father Nightroad. Don't waste time with extraneous tasks. Just focus on arresting the priest."

"No, we're not arresting the priest just yet, Major Iqus," a gruff voice answered. Radcon poked his fish-eyed face into the room. Bring back your men."

"My mission and your orders conflict. Please explain, Colonel," Tres requested as he placed his pistols back into their holsters. "I was ordered to arrest Father Nightroad. If we pursue him now, we will be able to capture him."

"Let the priest hang tight for a while. I received new orders from Lord Gyula," Radcon replied.

"Orders from Lord Gyula?" Tres asked.

"Nightroad seems to be an important piece in this case. He said to let him hang tight for a while. Besides . . ." Radcon ignored Tres and glanced over at Vitez. He looked her up and down, drooling. "Laura Vitez, you are under arrest for obstruction of justice and protecting terrorist suspect Nightroad. Major Iqus, arrest the rest of the clergy and take them to City Military Police headquarters. Once that is done, we will burn down the church."

†

"Telegram from Colonel Radcon. Saint Mathias Church under control, sir," a robot standing near the wall reported, but its master wasn't listening.

Gyula looked through the anti-UV glass window of his balcony to view the town of Pest. He noticed a thin trail of smoke rising at one end of the town as he remarked, "Finally. I finally made it."

How many years had it been since he had lost his beloved partner? Five years? Or was it a hundred? Though Methuselah lived for about three hundred years, a hundred years was a long time to be lonely, even for their kind.

His loneliness made him feel empty.

There was a large hole in his heart, something that would never be filled again. No matter how many times he avenged her death, his dearest love would never return.

But Gyula would not stop his revenge.

"The saying, 'Revenge will never create anything,' is foolish. A ridiculous statement made by one who has never loved anyone," Gyula scoffed. "Who uses revenge to create something? All those who seek revenge know their loved one will never return. The reason we seek revenge, staining our hands with blood, is to express our love through our victims' blood, screams, and fear . . . just one last time."

"Master, preparations for broadcast have been made," a robot announced. In the room, broadcast equipment was set up, waiting to be used.

Gyula came to. "Shall we begin?" He turned to face the wall painting behind him.

The woman in the painting sadly smiled back.

"Esther, are you all right?" Ignatz asked.

"Mister Ignatz, please call every one!" Esther said to the big man who opened the basement door. "It's an emergency! City Military Police attacked the church."

"Yes, we know! They were just announcing that on the radio. That's why we were worried about you," Ignatz said.

"On the radio?" Esther knit her brows. She noticed the group gathered around the table, listening intently to the radio in the center.

"We have confirmed the Vatican's organizational activities of destruction . . . the Marquis of Hungary . . . targeted . . . Father Abel Nightroad . . ."

The basement was deadly silent, but the radio voice was difficult to hear because of the static.

"Oh, they're talking about me," Abel said.

"I can't hear," Esther said. Someone raised the volume. When she was able to hear distinct sentences, Esther's brows raised.

"I say again. I am Gyula Kadar, the Marquis of Hungary, and of the oldest clan of Istavan. I declare to all of you: All citizens of Istavan and humankind are owned by the Marquis of Hungary. I declare the city of Istavan to be under my rule—starting now. I order City Council and the courts to close down immediately to prevent further confusion. Unlimited authority lies with me."

"N-no way. How can they declare that in public!" Esther exclaimed.

"Calm down, Esther. There's more. We need to know why the enemy is responding so fast," the tall priest interjected. Esther peered up at Abel's unusually calm face. He pushed up his glasses.

Just as the priest had predicted, the voice in the radio got straight to the point. *"We have confirmed the destructive activities of last night were caused by Father Nightroad of the Saint Mathias Church. We will make a formal protest to the Vatican, which ordered him to conduct these activities. We have closed down the Saint Mathias Church indefinitely and have arrested all the clergymen there."*

"Wh-what are they talking about?" Esther stammered.

Closed the church? Arrested the clergymen? She clearly understood the radio's announcement but refused to believe it. They took over the city, closed down the church, arrested the clergy, and accused the Vatican of running terrorist operations.

"Oh God, what in the world?" Dietrich gasped.

"The vampires are picking a fight with the Vatican!" the others exclaimed.

Caterina Sforza, beautiful in her scarlet cardinal's robe, muttered, "Oh God, what is going on?"

The blinking red and white lights along a border on the eastern area map indicated the rapid movements of both the Vatican military and the Istavan City Military Police.

Reports from several priests came in.

"The Tenth Armored Infantry Battalion, Saint Stefan Knights, appear to be receiving fire from Istavan City Military Police armored vehicles! Request to engage!" stated one.

"We lost signal from the patrol balloon heading for the fourth sector! Possibly shot down!" reported another.

"Incoming message from the air battleship *Ramiel* patrolling the border! *'Confirmed Istavan's armed military ship, Knights of the Dragon the* Charkane, *at two zero nine dash zero three seven. No response to our heeds. Awaiting orders.'* Over!" said another.

"No! Are the Istavan vampires trying to start a war with the Vatican?!" Francesco exploded. His opinion represented the views of the high-ranking clergy gathered at San Angelo Castle.

Over the past several hundred years, the powerful Vatican was the center of the universe and humankind. Recently, the nobles and common people had become more arrogant, but never did they try to go against the Vatican. What was that lonely free city thinking? On top of that, how dare a Methuselah declare control over humans?

The cardinals whispered to each other, more confused than scared.

"So, what is the overall strength of the enemy?"

"We confirmed two or three regular infantry regiments— roughly two- or three-thousand strong. Also, one mechanized battalion is equipped with Germanic tanks and armored vehicles, and one armored infantry company equipped with Germanic armored suits and mechanized soldiers. In addition, they have one squadron of airships with one destroyer and two frigates."

"If that's all they've got, our border patrol can take care of them. We won't need any reinforcements."

"Well, seems like the Istavan vampires are getting desperate."

Among the whispering, Francesco's loud voice announced, "This is the chance we've been waiting for!" He violently pounded the table. "They are the ones who started this battle. This gives us the justification to invade. Let's order the knights and air squadrons to move in! We can finish them off in three days!"

Caterina silently listened to her half brother's suggestion and his supporters' comments.

The situation was too good to be true. It was as if someone offered the Vatican a reason to conduct military operations. With such obvious threats, even Caterina and her conservative supporters could not argue against the decision to deploy forces. She probably would be hanged if she even dared to speak of other options.

"Is the Marquis of Hungary hoping for the Empire's support?" Caterina wondered. *No, that can't be the reason.*

The New Human Empire definitely was the greatest threat to mankind, but over the past hundred years, they had avoided conflict with humans. With that in mind, it would be hard to believe that the Empire would opt to fight the Vatican over a small city on their border.

Then there is only one other reason. The weapon that the agents reported. The Star of Sorrow . . . We should've destroyed it while we had the chance, Caterina thought.

What, exactly, the weapon could do was unknown, but it must be powerful enough if the Marquis of Hungary wanted to start a war. It would be foolish to leave it alone. Should an agent try to sabotage it?

"Sister, u-u-um . . ." a feeble voice said with a whimper. Her younger half brother shivered as he watched Caterina deep in thought. "Um, wh-wh-what should I d-do? If we wa-wage a w-w-war, d-do I have to g-go?"

"Don't worry, Alec. You can stay in Rome. Definitely." Caterina smiled to reassure the Pope.

"Th-the Saint Mathias Chapel has been attacked by Istavan City Military Police!"

That was the most alarming news of the night.

An intelligence agency priest continued to report the tragic incident, "The church has been raided and burnt to the ground! Bishop Vitez and thirty-three clergymen were kidnapped by City Military Police. We have not confirmed their safety yet!"

THE BE†RAYING KNIGH†

*Their tongue is as an arrow shot out;
it speaketh deceit: one speaketh
peaceably to his neighbor with his
mouth, but in heart he layeth his wait.*
—Jeremiah 9:8

I

A line of orange light beamed across the cloudy sky. It was the illuminated trail of a handmade rocket, launched into the palace's center court. It sounded like thunder when it exploded on impact.

"Seems like Dietrich's begun," Esther observed through her binoculars. From her vantage point on Pest's riverside, it was easy to see the action in Buda.

The bombs set up in various locations within the palace went off, one after another. The sleepy soldiers were awakened and groggily came to the scene. They probably didn't expect an attack on the castle owned by the Marquis of Hungary. The soldiers could only react helplessly to the bombs, as Dietrich exploded each in perfect rhythm. It was a great plan.

Esther passed the binoculars to the side. She felt wary but satisfied. On the west side of the river, where Pest was located, there was a large building with a purple-brown dome on top that was surrounded by white pinnacles. It was the old council building but now acted as City Military Police headquarters. More than half the military was deployed to the border to fight the Vatican; but the First Regiment, led by Colonel Radcon, guarded the city.

The strongest regiment responded quickly. Within the first five minutes of the bombings, soldiers mounted their armored vehicles and quickly headed to the west side of town.

"I want to go over the plan once more," Esther said, lowering her binoculars before turning to her comrades.

In the dusty room, men and women of all ages were holding crude weapons. Other than a few people assisting Dietrich in the deception plan, this group contained all the Partisans.

"Right now, we are here." Esther pointed to the map on the wall.

They were in an old museum annex, which was built before the Armageddon. It used to be a beautiful edifice lined with tiles and graceful curves, but it was now just a crumbling, abandoned building. After the Armageddon, this part of Pest never was redeveloped, so it had remained uninhabited for a long time.

This was one of the relay points Esther used to conduct Partisan activities. They appropriated the old subway tunnel system to access various parts of town.

"From here, we will use the eighth subway route to reach the police's headquarters, more than two-hundred sixty feet underground," Esther explained.

"Is the underground headquarters truly located there?" one of the squad leaders asked.

Esther nodded in response. "There's a holding place for political criminals, as well. The advance party is creating an entranceway through one of the walls. Once the excavation is complete, the first squad and I will go rescue the bishop and her clergy. Imure's eighth squad will be in charge of evacuating the rescued people. We must safely transport them out of the city, no matter what," Esther emphasized.

"Gotcha," said a gray-haired old man before biting on his pipe. The crowd nodded in unison. Once they led the clergy out of town, a horse caravan could take them to the Vatican military.

The Partisans weren't saving Bishop Vitez and her clergy out of sentimentality alone—they also wanted to avoid having the clergy used as hostages to compromise the Vatican.

"The other squads will conduct additional deception plans inside the police headquarters," Esther explained.

"Oh, what we do all the time," someone remarked. The whole group laughed.

Esther cracked a smile for a moment; then she returned to serious business.

"But please don't stay around too long. The military police at the palace might come back if that happens. The time is now eighteen hundred. We will execute at eighteen thirty. Regardless of the results, please retreat no later than nineteen hundred. Is that understood?" Esther asked.

"Yeah!" everyone raised their crude rifles and yelled in unison; then they prepared for action. Each squad leader inspected their squads and disappeared into the subway tunnels.

Esther saw off the departing squads, feeling nervousness mixed with fear. Her heart ached.

How many of them will make it back alive?

She knew that they had to fight; it was now or never. The Vatican military supposedly had started their invasion. The Marquis of Hungary, lacking military power, surely would use the clergy as human shields against the Vatican. Then the fight would continue, and more lives would be lost. This was a battle to prevent a huge loss of life—a small fight to end the large one. It was not wrong.

But her heart still ached.

Her comrades listened to her directions, willingly risking their lives. Was she just an angel of death? She motivated them to fight, but wasn't she responsible if they were to die?

"Er, Sister Esther?" a lax voice asked, interrupting her thoughts. "How far is it to City Military Police headquarters? I hope it's not too far because, you know, I'm from the city. I haven't walked much," Abel fretted.

Listening to his out-of-place complaint, Esther forgot her worries. She looked back at Abel, who was walking right behind her. "Umm, I'd rather have you stay back at this point instead of coming with us, Father."

"Well, I'd like to do that, too, but . . ." Abel answered sadly, almost sobbing. "But if I make it back to Rome safely without participating, it will affect my career. They'll accuse me of leaving behind my peers. The Vatican is pretty picky about that sort of thing," Abel explained.

"But, you're aware of the danger involved, right?" Esther asked him.

"Yes, of course. But could you please take me, anyway? When we get there, I promise to hide behind your back the whole time," Abel answered.

"I guess." Esther smiled wryly. "Then please follow me. Try not to get separated."

"Yes, of course. I will stay quiet the whole time. Don't worry," Abel said with a serious face.

Esther almost broke out in laughter at the sight. His comical nature eased the pain in her heart a bit.

"Let's go then!" Esther held the rosary cross and led her squad, including Ignatz. "May the Lord be with you!"

II

Hey, how are things over here?" a soldier asked.

"No problems so far." Private Second Class Schtindle pulled the rifle sling from his shoulder as he replied to his replacement. "What happened to the fight up there?" The basement facility he was guarding used to be a nuclear shelter. It was well lit with fluorescent lamps, but it had bad ventilation, causing cold air to come in.

Schtindle blew puffs of white mist when he breathed.

"It's a matter of time. They're so stupid to fight head on, instead of pulling guerrilla tactics like they usually do," his replacement answered.

"No, not about them. I meant the Vatican. How far did they come?" Schtindle whispered. The Vatican's response to Lord Gyula's declaration of war was swift. It was as if they had positioned their forces at the border before the announcement. "The Vatican military is the strongest force in the world. Will we be okay?" Schtindle asked.

"Yeah, I didn't expect our boss to pick a fight with them. Speaking of which, our boss is quite a monster," his replacement commented.

"Hush! Don't say that out loud!" Schtindle hissed, but he did agree with the man.

Schtindle left his hometown to escape charges of robbery, murder, and rape; he'd ended up in Istavan six months ago. For a heavy duty criminal, City Military Police was heaven. He had all the money and women he wanted, and he could push around the townspeople to blow off steam. Schtindle didn't care if his boss wasn't human, as long as he could keep doing as he pleased. But he didn't expect his boss to go against the Vatican! Why the Vatican?

Maybe it's time to leave this place, Schtindle thought, recalling the location of his secret stash of money and jewelry.

Behind him, a voiced called out, "Hey, good job!" It was a really skinny soldier.

He was walking bow-legged, dragging his longer-than-usual coat in a very un-soldierlike manner. Behind his thick glasses, his winter-blue eyes twinkled "Er, um, good morning. It's cold, because it's winter, and winter is cold."

"Who the hell are you?" the two soldiers asked.

Was he really in City Military Police?

The two soldiers glared suspiciously at the tall young man as he hobbled toward them, smiling awkwardly.

"Wait, stop right there! Who are you?"

"Er, um, well, I'm here to replace you," Abel replied.

"Replace? Stupid, we were just about to turn over . . . Hey!" Schtindle stopped in mid-sentence. He recognized the tall, clumsy man from before. "He's that priest—ack!"

A thick arrow pierced Schtindle's hand. His buddy fell to ground, screaming, as the same type of arrow pierced his leg.

"Don't move!" a girl's voice yelled.

"P-Partisan!" Schtindle barked.

From underneath Abel's coat, the girl appeared, holding a crossbow.

"H-how did you guys get in?!" Schtindle asked, but didn't receive an answer. Instead, a blunted arrow shot right between his eyes. It didn't kill him, but it knocked him out cold.

"You're mean, Esther! I told you I wanted to hide behind you," Abel complained.

"I'll listen to your complaints later! We need to hurry!" Esther shot down his objections and whistled. She fished through the keys hanging from the unconscious soldier's hip. Partisans entered the room one after the other. She threw the ring of keys to a large man and yelled, "Ignatz, hurry! The bishop and her people are over there!"

From the other end of the hallway, gunshots and yelling echoed. A different group was engaging the police. There was no time to waste: Even the time spent turning the key felt long. But when the door screeched open halfway, everyone jumped inside.

Partisan voices yelled out in the dark.

"It's dark in here. Turn on the lights!"

"Watch out! There might be other guards!"

"Bishop, we came to rescue you!"

A small house would have fit into the large room they'd entered; but there were no lights, so it was hard to see. Prison bars wrapped around the room, and a rank smell, worse than the stench of sweat and blood, filled the area.

"Bishop, where are you? Please answer me!" Esther called out.

"Sorry, but . . ." a strong male voice answered from the high ceilings above. It was gentle, yet thick, like heavy alcohol. "We regret to inform you that Bishop Vitez is not here. Welcome."

All the lights came on, temporarily blinding the Partisans' vision. They covered their eyes and stepped back. When their eyes adjusted, they noticed the catwalk—filled with armed men.

"Police!" a Partisan yelled.

About fifty soldiers were standing above them, but what really scared the Partisans were not those who wore dark blue uniforms. Rather, they were shocked at the sight of one man standing among the soldiers. He wore a black coat and had curly black hair and gray eyes. Fangs protruded from his mouth.

"Gyu-Gyula Kadar!" Esther shrieked. "Wh-why are you here, Marquis?"

"Is it really surprising to find me here, Sister Esther?" Gyula snickered. He bowed to her as if he were a gentleman meeting a lady in the ballroom. "I am indeed Gyula Kadar, the Marquis of Hungary. Are you Star? I'm surprised to find hat the terrorist leader is such a beautiful young lady."

Esther glared back at the sneering marquis. "I screwed up!"

The plan had somehow leaked. The clergy were not here; and with so few comrades, escape would be impossible.

"Let's surrender, Esther," a small voice behind her suggested. "We'll just lay down our weapons and let them arrest us."

"No, Father! If we get caught, the bishop and her clergy . . ." Esther trailed off.

"Don't you understand? That's exactly why we should let them arrest us." Abel shook his head and pushed his glasses up his nose. His voice was surprisingly calm and collected. "They didn't shoot us when we first entered; that means they don't intend to kill us yet. They'll probably use us as hostages along with the bishop and her clergy. So the possibility that they'll lock us up in the same place is rather high."

"I see," Esther said. There was no way her group could fight their way out alive or save Bishop Vitez here. But if they surrendered, it was likely that they'd be taken to Bishop Vitez and the other hostages. It would be better to plan an escape once they were with the others.

"We give up, Marquis." Esther choked on her words, hoping none of her comrades would shoot in haste. She placed her crossbow on the ground and slumped her shoulders. "We surrender, so please don't shoot."

"A commendable decision." Gyula chuckled and stepped off the catwalk, dropping down at least sixteen feet without displacing a single strand of hair.

Gyula took large catlike steps toward Esther; then he and lifted her chin with his fingers.

"Seventeen or eighteen years old, perhaps?" Gyula snarled, regarding her white face. "I don't understand, Terran. Why would you want to risk your life at such a young age? Or is your kind a stupid breed?"

"We don't want to risk our lives if we don't have to. But . . ." Esther looked up at the handsome, inhuman creature. If he simply flicked one of his fingernails resting under her chin, he could easily cut open her throat. A cold sweat trailed down her back.

"But we risk our lives when it counts—such as for our family. Doesn't your kind feel the same way, Marquis?" Esther asked carefully.

"Well, there's nobody that I consider family, unfortunately, so I wouldn't know," Gyula answered nonchalantly, letting go of Esther's chin. He looked at Abel, who stood behind Esther.

"Oh, is that you, Father Nightroad? I was quite upset that you left so early last night. I wondered if you didn't appreciate my hospitality," Gyula said.

"I apologize for troubling you." Abel bowed in response. "But, sir, you are quite cunning. You used me as bait at the train station to draw in the Partisans, right? In fact, you tried to place the blame on the terrorists and the church."

"There's nothing wrong with blaming those who are truly guilty." Gyula sneered, not denying the accusation. "In fact, aren't you trying to kill me, AX Agent Abel Nightroad?"

Esther didn't recognize the title, so she inadvertently looked back at Abel, who tensed his face and stayed silent.

"Where are the bishop and the clergy?" one of the Partisans blurted. "Where did you put Bishop Vitez and the others?"

Gyula returned to the main subject. "Oh, by the way, I need to give you something, Sister Esther." He pulled out something from his coat pocket: It was a rosary covered in blood and dirt, a rosary that Esther recognized immediately.

"Th-that's the bishop's!" Esther stammered.

Gyula took her hand and placed the rosary in her palm. He whispered into her ear, "I killed her."

Her brain couldn't accept that statement. Esther stood there, frozen from shock. She could take only shallow breaths.

Gyula, entertained by her reaction, stated, "You were a bit too late, Sister Esther. Last night, I gave that woman and the others their death sentence."

Esther screamed like a wild animal. She pulled out a knife from under her arm and kicked the ground.

"No! Stop, Esther!" the priest tried to intervene. He touched her shoulder, but she slipped away.

Esther dashed toward the vampire, aiming straight for his face.

"Hmph!" Gyula swatted away the knife and the girl with one swing of his mighty arm. His ring clanged against the knife for a moment. The girl was flung into the air. She somehow landed on her feet like a feline, still grasping the knife. Once again, she headed toward the vampire, this time aiming for his solar plexus.

"A lady shouldn't hold such a dangerous object." The vampire snickered while the girl cried out in pain. Not only did Gyula dodge Esther's attack, but he grabbed both her hand and the knife. "Why don't you act more ladylike?!"

Esther slammed into the ground. If Abel hadn't slid under Esther to break her fall, her skull would have cracked open.

Abel yelled, "Esther!"

One of the Partisans raised his rifle and hastily shot a round. It nicked Gyula's cheek but ricocheted off the wall behind him, flying over the other Partisans' heads.

"Hey, watch it!" Ignatz yelled as he took the young man's rifle away from him. "Close quarters battle! It's now or never, you guys!"

"Firing is not authorized, lest it hit the Marquis of Hungary! Fix bayonets!" the police officer bellowed to his men. "Charge!"

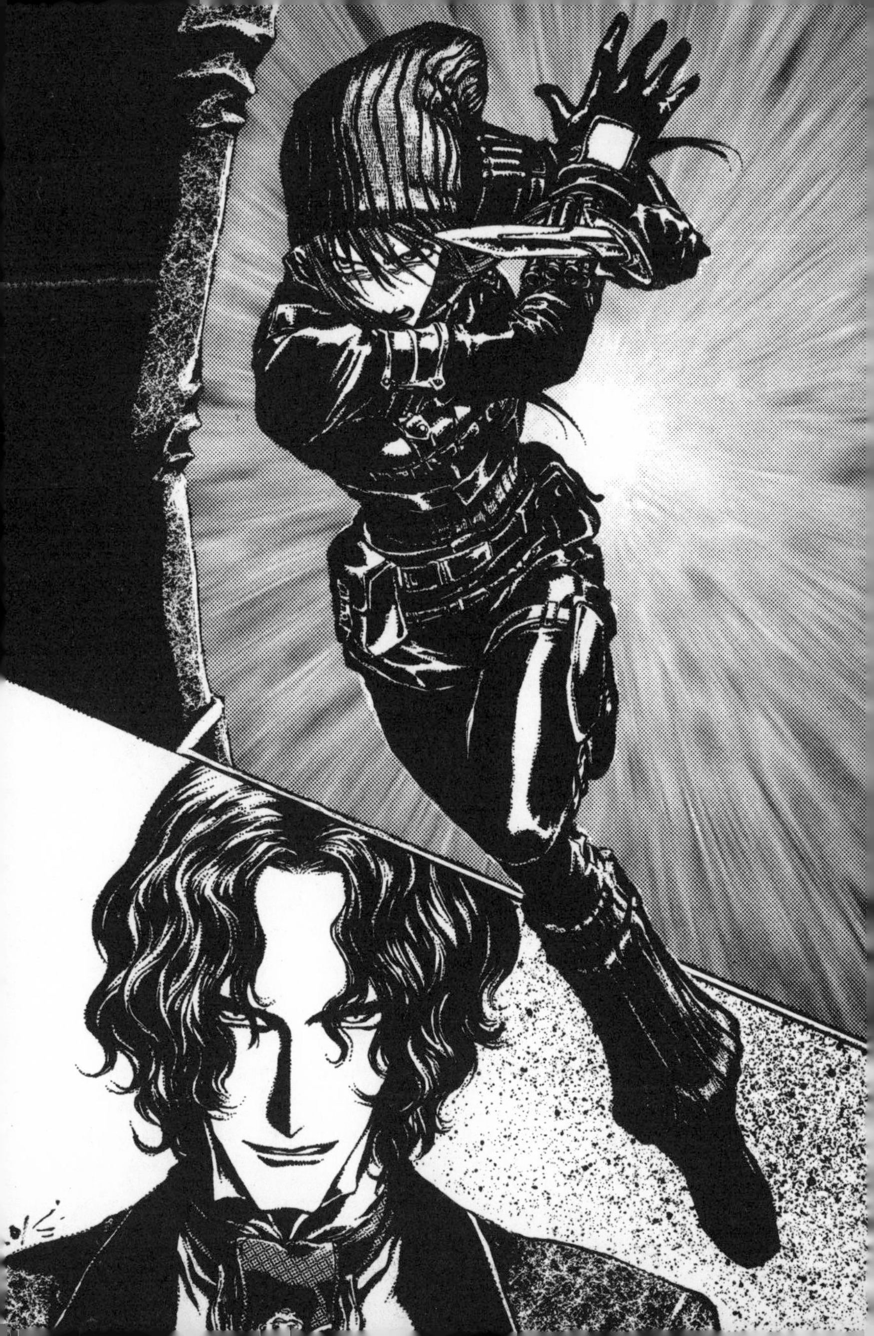

White flashes projected on the ground and ceiling. In an attempt to save their leader, the Partisans raised their knives and axes to attack the vampire. The soldiers, trying to prevent it, jumped off the catwalk; their rifles ready. The two groups yelled war cries as they clashed.

"Go to hell, Gyula!" A young man gripped the muzzle end of his rifle and swung the walnut buttstock like a bat at the vampire's forehead.

Some of the Partisans exclaimed, "Is he down?!" The buttstock swung where Gyula's forehead was supposed to be. "H-he's gone?!"

The buttstock smacked into the wall and splintered the plaster. The young man covered his face to block the flying chunks of plaster.

Gyula remarked, "What a crude weapon. Did you think you could kill me with this?"

The young man's face contorted when realized that Gyula had ripped the rifle from his hands.

The vampire stopped using haste mode; he grinned at the young man as he said, "You can have it back."

Gyula flicked his wrist. The next moment, the dry sound of bone crushing was followed by the wet sound of flesh tearing. The hunting rifle pierced through the young man's chest, ripping out a chunk of his heart, which was crushed into the wall behind him. The rifle pinned the young man like a needle through an insect specimen.

One of the Partisans went berserk at the death of a comrade and fired his gun repeatedly. "Y-you bastard!" he raged.

Gyula used haste mode again to avoid the shots, so the rounds missed him. Unfortunately, they made holes in a Partisan comrade before ricocheting up to break one of the ceiling lamps.

"Esther! Esther! Please get up!" Abel shook Esther amid the bloodshed and cries. She still was unresponsive from her fall.

"Father, take Esther and get away!" Ignatz yelled. "The operation was a failure! We'll hold them down! Take Esther and get out!" Ignatz hollered, his belly shaking.

"B-but, Ignatz," Abel tried to protest, but then he bit his lip. The Partisans were being mowed down like grass. There was no way they could win. Abel picked up Esther under his left arm, turned around one last time, and said, "Thank you, Ignatz. Good luck!"

"Gotcha, Father! Please help Esther!" Ignatz yelled back.

Abel bit his lip and ran out, carrying Esther. Though he was holding the girl, he sped out faster than anyone expected.

But another shadow ran next to him at the same speed.

"No lowly Terran can escape me, Father Nightroad!" Gyula's gray eyes glinted. The next moment, a violent wind ripped through. An extremely fast-moving object whipped toward Abel, who was running at normal speed. A sharp bone protruded out of Gyula's fist as he tried to strike Abel with the back of his hand.

"F-Father!" one of the Partisans yelled.

It looked like Gyula's bone blade had slashed Abel. The Partisans, sensing their leader in danger, pointed their muzzles at Gyula. But the humans couldn't possibly see the vampire in haste mode, so they'd just assumed that Abel was down.

"What?!" Gyula exclaimed as he jumped back. In place of the expected red blood spray, white, thundering flashes of gunfire filled the room.

With his right hand, Abel had pulled out his percussion revolver and fired. White smoke rose from the muzzle.

Gyula jumped high, swiftly dodging the bullets before landing on the wall. He glared, baring his fangs and scowling. "How dare you, Father Nightroad?!"

Abel fired again, cutting off Gyula's scowl. Though Abel was carrying Esther, his aim was deadly accurate.

"Urk!" Gyula grunted.

Switching back to haste mode, Gyula barely dodged two rounds, which scraped his hair. The shiny bullets traced a white path, a unique characteristic of silver-tipped bullets—something almost as deadly as ultraviolet rays to Methuselah. But the rounds were useless unless the silver actually came in contact with the vampire—made more difficult because vampires in haste mode were the fastest creatures on Earth.

Gyula smiled wickedly at Abel, who seemed immobile. He kicked out to leap toward the priest. "Gah!" Gyula groaned as he slammed into the ground.

"Dammit, AX Agent . . . You putrid Terran!" he raged. He felt pain run down his back. The two rounds Abel fired had scraped Gyula's back and dug into the wall behind him. They happened to hit the heater's steam pipe.

Even Methuselah, who were almost invincible and recovered faster than humans, couldn't bear having high-pressured, hot steam burning them.

This bought Abel some time. The priest held his empty revolver and the unconscious girl in his arms as he dashed away from the vampire's screams.

III

Voices yelled out while military boots pounded the ground in the tunnels, which were lighted by fluorescent lamps.

"You find them?!"

"No, not over here. Where did they disappear?"

The troops were searching for two escapees and the other remaining Partisans. A low, grumbling voice, bellowed, "Second platoon, go to Sector B! First platoon, follow me! We're going to sweep the warehouse area again!" Radcon turned around and retraced his steps. One of the platoons followed him.

Though the men scanned the ground and things at their eye level, nobody seemed to notice the air duct openings in the ceiling. A small, round glow coming from one of the air ducts went unnoticed.

Abel stayed quietly in place until a little after the growling voice and stomping boots faded out. After confirming that they were gone, he retreated farther into the air duct.

He crouched forward and turned into one of the side openings.

It was a hallway that probably had been used as an electrical maintenance passageway. Abel, avoiding the fluorescent lamps that hung from above, carefully stood up.

"Well, this is rough. We're completely surrounded. The others might've been arrested or they could have escaped successfully.

Until things settle down, we should lie low here," Abel tried to say pleasantly. "It'll be okay. They won't find us here, and will give up eventually. After that, we'll get out of here and meet up with the others, right?"

"Is there anyone left to meet up with?" the girl asked in a depressed manner, sitting with her knees hugged up to her chest. It seemed like all the life had been sucked out of her. She peered down at the ground with her usually sparkling eyes now as dull as a cheap doll's. Her face was hard, betraying no emotions. "All of them probably got caught or killed, like the bishop," she groaned.

"Don't think like that, Esther." Abel placed his cape across Esther's shoulder and shook his head. "Don't say such things. You don't know for sure if the others were arrested or killed. Some of them might have escaped. Oh, yes! Dietrich's group might be okay, too," Abel tried to reassure her.

"Stop that!" The girl covered her ears and shrieked hysterically. "I dragged everyone into this mess. If only I hadn't done this. I killed the bishop and the clergy!"

"Regardless of whether you or I were involved with the Partisans, the Marquis of Hungary would have attacked the church eventually. For some reason, he despises it. It's not your fault that the church was attacked and the clergy killed," Abel responded.

"But if I would've been more careful, I could've escorted the bishop and the clergy out of this town safely," Esther muttered.

"That wasn't possible. You know that. Esther, stop blaming yourself for everything. We don't have much time. Please focus on what you need to do," Abel pleaded.

"Focus on what I need to do?" Esther repeated. She didn't even think of that. She had to save her captured comrades before they ended up like Bishop Vitez—but how?

"It's impossible, Father." Esther shook her head and looked down once more. "There's no one left. I can't fight anymore."

"No one left? Esther, have you forgotten your most powerful ally?" Abel inquired.

"Eh?" Esther wondered.

Esther looked up to see the priest's face, and noticed that he was smiling and confidently pointing at himself. "Me! I'm your most powerful ally!" Abel declared.

Esther looked blankly at Abel's blustering confidence. She was fishing for words in vain. Both stared at each other in silence for while.

"Um, this is embarrassing," Abel finally commented.

"Pfft," Esther held back her laughter as she ducked to hide her reddened face.

Abel was offended by her reaction and rolled his eyes, saying, "How rude! I'm trying to help you, and you mock me!"

"B-but, but . . ." Esther tried to respond, but she laughed so hard that she shook. She giggled like a typical seventeen-year-old.

Abel looked at her tenderly. It was his first time hearing her truly laugh since he arrived in town.

After Esther stopped laughing, she said, "Thank you, Father." She stood up, patting her sleeves. She still looked a bit tired and pale, but the sparkle in her eyes had returned.

It was time to go. There was no time to feel sorry for themselves.

"Let's go. If we stay here with everyone out there waiting for us, we might put them in worse danger," Esther said.

"Yes, that's true. Shall we continue through this passageway? I hope this connects to the subway tunnels," Abel suggested.

"If so, then we should go that way." Esther breathed out puffs of white air as she led Abel. The small passageway had a low ceiling and many twists and turns; but as there was only one way out, they couldn't get lost.

"Oh, Father, may I ask you a question?" Esther asked while briskly walking.

"Yes, what is it?" Abel responded.

"What is AX? And an AX agent?" Esther inquired.

Abel paused. Esther didn't know whether he was silent because he was concentrating on not hitting his head on the ceiling or for another reason.

Esther repeated the question, "The Marquis of Hungary called you 'AX Agent.' What's that?" Esther's question was simply out of curiosity. That's why Abel's serious response was totally unexpected.

"Esther, I have to tell you the truth," Abel said.

"Eh?" Esther stopped and turned. She noticed the serious look on his face. "Wh-what's wrong, Father Nightroad? Why the serious look?"

Abel stayed silent and tried to find the right words. After a few moments, he took a deep breath and confessed, "Esther, I'm not actually a priest."

"Huh?" Esther was confused. *If he isn't a priest, then what can he be?*

Abel continued, "I'm not a priest. I'm really . . ."

"AX Agent Abel Nightroad. Code name Crusnik. That's who he is," a voice called out. "AX is the Vatican's Papal State Affairs Special Operations Section. The Vatican's spy agency. He's a spy."

"D-Dietrich!" Esther called out to the shadowed, wobbling figure. She ran to Dietrich, shocked to see his injuries. "Dietrich, you're hurt! Where are the others?!"

"They got us good. They captured everyone and squeezed information out of them. That's why your plan leaked," Dietrich gasped, barely standing. His handsome face was pale, his clothes were tattered, and the gun he was holding was covered in blood. The bandage around his forehead also was drenched in blood.

He glared with disgust at Abel and pointed a gun at him.

"Just sit down, Dietrich! Let me treat your injuries," Esther tried to offer.

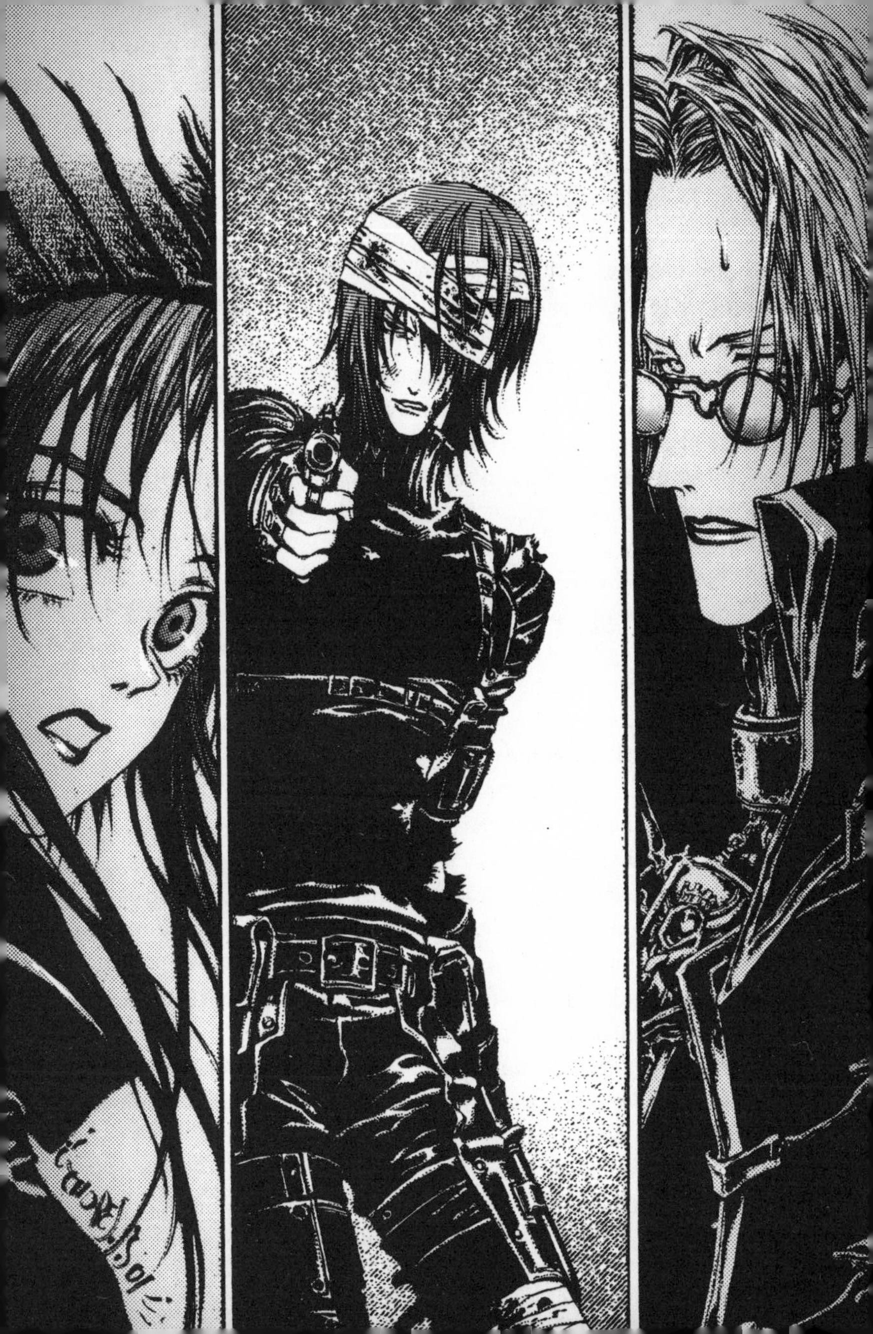

"Forget my injuries! We need to deal with him!" Dietrich's arm was quaking, and he had difficulty aiming at Abel. But it was obvious he was trying to shoot the priest.

"I've had my suspicions. First, he went to Gyula's estate without hesitation; then, City Military Police pretty much ambushed us at the church right when we got there. Today—why did City Military Police know all our plans?" Dietrich deducted, "There was a mole among us! Father Nightroad, you must have leaked information to them! Just to stir things up!"

"Um, Dietrich, please calm down," Abel said.

"Yes, Dietrich. Why would Father Nightroad do such a thing? I don't know what an AX agent is, but there's no proof of that yet," Esther said.

"Proof? This is proof!" Dietrich took Esther's hand and slapped an envelope in her palm. The envelope was charred in several places, but the letter inside was intact.

"This morning, when I attacked the Valley of Blood, I found this. It's the Vatican's personnel file. Gyula probably used his spy to obtain it," Dietrich continued.

It was stationery similar to that Esther used to see on Bishop Vitez's desk when she cleaned the woman's office, a memo the church normally used.

But the contents revealed: "Abel Nightroad. Birthdate: Unknown. Height: Unknown. Weight: Unknown. Background: Unknown," Esther read.

Most of the information was marked 'unknown.' At the bottom of the memo, though, was a peculiar sentence.

"It says 'currently unavailable for communications due to the execution of covert operations in Istavan.' Wh-what does this mean?" Esther asked.

"Don't you get it, Esther? He's a Vatican pawn! He's here to stir things up to instigate a reason for the Vatican to invade this city! He leaked information to Gyula to do so!" Dietrich explained.

"Th-that's not true, Dietrich. I'm not a spy!" Abel took a step back and shook his head. His eyes swam behind his glasses and his face flushed. "Esther, that's not true! I was trying to prevent a war."

"Father," Esther swallowed. She didn't want to hear that.

"I am your ally," Abel said to her.

He was trying to support her in her hour of need. But she had to ask . . . "Father," Esther said in a shaky voice. "Are you a Roman spy? Were you sent here by the AX section?"

Abel looked at Esther with sorrow. Esther almost felt like it was *she* who had betrayed *him*.

But he gave her the answer she didn't want to hear. "Yes. I am AX Agent Abel Nightroad. I came to this town to conduct a special mission for the Vatican."

"So you tricked us the whole time. You acted like a priest, and then you pretended to be goofy,. You fooled the bishop, the others, and me . . ." Esther calmly accused him, suppressing her anger. "You had us fooled the whole time!"

"N-no! Esther, that's not true!" Abel pleaded.

"I don't want to hear your excuses! It's your fault that the bishop . . . the bishop . . ." Esther sobbed.

"Shoot him, Esther! Shoot the traitor, for everyone's sake!" Dietrich handed the gun to Esther and urged her. "Esther, you're right! Avenge the bishop's death!"

Esther stopped.

"'Avenge the bishop's death?' Dietrich, how do you know she died?" Esther's voice quivered. She held the gun in her hand and said, "Please answer. I just heard about the bishop's death a few minutes ago. And you weren't there when the vampire told us. How could you know about it?"

Dietrich, still tired, just stared at Esther. Esther was hoping to hear a reassuring reason from Dietrich.

"Oh man, that's why I hate clever girls," Dietrich sighed. Fatigue disappeared from Dietrich's handsome face. He stood up straight, looking like a different person entirely. He had an evil glint in his eyes. It was as if he'd switched personalities while looking at Esther.

Esther sensed the difference and subconsciously reacted by pointing the gun at him. "Don't move! I'll shoot if you move!" Esther said.

"Are you trying to shoot me?" Dietrich snickered. "Please, I dare you."

"I mean it!" Esther squeezed the trigger. Of course, she meant it to be a warning shot, so she pointed away from him.

But right after the gunshot came a muffled groan.

"Huh?" Esther was surprised. When she opened her eyes, she noticed Abel stepping back and grabbing his right shoulder. He winced in pain.

"E-Esther," Abel stammered.

"Wh-why?" Esther stuttered as she looked at her own hand, which was aiming the gun straight toward the priest. In her eyes, she saw her own finger squeeze the trigger again.

Another gunshot. This time, it hit the priest's left shoulder.

"Wh-why?! Why?!" Esther cried. *Why did my fingers and hand move on their own?!*

Esther desperately tried to shake the gun from her hand. But her hand refused to obey; instead, it gripped the gun harder.

"Oh, it's no use trying to control it, Esther. When I touched you, I implanted a string similar to this one," Dietrich explained as he watched Esther's confusion with glee. A very thin string shined between his fingers. It probably was only a few microns thick. It was so thin that it was barely visible.

"This is one the lost technologies that I found. It's a very thin living fiber. When transplanted on the skin, it digs in and fuses to the human nerves, and then it sends out electrical impulses on its own. Like this," Dietrich continued.

The gun fired again.

Abel fell down to one knee as the round pierced his thigh.

"F-Father!" Esther screamed as she saw her hand move on its own again. "Father! Father! Noooo!"

"What a good scream. Oh, I made it so you still have control of your head. You can scream and cry all you want." Dietrich sighed in pleasure. "I was waiting for the day you'd scream like this. It was a long wait, but it was worth it to hear your very pretty cries."

"Why? Why are you . . . ?" Esther hoarsely asked Dietrich, her eyes and gun pointed toward the priest. She wanted to help Abel up, but her body refused to move. She could only turn her head toward Dietrich as she asked again, "Why did you betray us? Why are you doing this?!"

"The primary reason is business. The Marquis of Hungary is my client," Dietrich answered.

He reached out and wiped Esther's tears from her cheeks with his finger. He leaned over and whispered to her like a lover would, "And the other reason is: I really liked you, Esther."

Dietrich licked Esther's tears from his finger and smiled innocently. He continued, "You know how boys tease girls they like? That's what I did. You were the most foolish girl I'd ever met. Even though you're powerless, you always spoke of justice. You were loved by everyone around you since you were born, and never thinking anyone possibly could hate your guts. I just wanted to toy with an utterly blissful and foolish girl like you."

"You did all this just for that?" Esther stood there, frozen. She did her best to glare back at the monster. "You betrayed us just to do this?! You devil!"

"What a great word! But you still don't seem to understand your situation yet," Dietrich commented.

Esther arched back and shrieked. A burning sensation ran along her nerves. Her body refused to fall to the ground, so she stood in place, crying out from the burning pain.

"This string isn't connected only to your motor nerves. It's also connected to your senses. Your whole nervous system is under my control," Dietrich explained. He moved his fingers nonchalantly and continued, "So, what do you want to feel? Would you like to feel all kinds of torture at once? I won't stop your heart. I wonder what you'd feel when all the pain runs through your body? When you're on the brink of dying from shock? Or would you like to feel pleasure? How would you like the feel of ten men playing with your body? How many seconds can you hold back before writhing in filthy pleasure?"

Though Esther was in pain already, Dietrich continued to torment her. He placed a hand on her shoulder and looked at the fallen priest as if he remembered something. "Oh, I'll have you play the most torturous game," he remarked.

"N-no, please!" Esther screamed as she realized what Dietrich was trying to make her do. But her finger already pulled the trigger several times.

The rounds hit the priest's shoulder. Abel couldn't even yell.

"Father!" Esther cried, trying in vain to stop her hand. Her arm aimed at a different part of the priest's body and pulled the trigger again.

"N-no," Esther whimpered. She feared what she was about to do. "Please, stop."

"No way," Dietrich refused.

The last bullet fired.

THE S✦AR ⊕F S⊕RR⊕W

*The light of the sun broke
forth; the lowly were exalted
and they devoured the nobles.*
—Book of Esther, Prologue 1:10

I

Don't look so sad. It's almost over. I'm almost done with having the people pay for what they did to you," Gyula said to the smiling woman in the portrait. He dropped a tablet into his drink.

The dime-sized blood tablet fizzled in the glass, making Methuselah Life Water. The wine turned from a thin, transparent ruby to a thick, opaque scarlet. He seemed uninterested as he swirled the drink in the wine glass and drank it.

His thirst was satiated. His pale face regained its color.

Gyula didn't like the taste of blood because it smelled raw, felt too thick when swallowed and had a horrible aftertaste. Blood tablets mixed into wine tasted better.

Adding some extra perfume and opium gave it an exquisite flavor. But this thirst was a minor irritant. Methuselah had an average life span of three hundred years, unsurpassed vitality, and an almost perfect immune system—but they were compelled to satisfy their thirst, which resulted from the only defect in their bodies, a congenital, chronic anemia. Their periodic loss of red blood cells drove them to thirst for blood; and during these attacks, even vampires with a strong will lost control of their minds. Once a Methuselah lost control, nothing could stop him. Unlike modern times, when anyone easily could acquire blood tablets, their ancestors literally had to live off blood to quench their thirst. It was no wonder the humans called them vampires back then. But Gyula didn't like that name at all now.

He drank all the liquid, placed the glass on the table, and passed through the center court to get to the balcony.

Surrounded by gray, anti-UV glass windows, he saw the sun set in the west. As the white-hot orb gradually sank and the sky also grew dark, the two moons glowed brighter.

"Pardon me. Dietrich von Lohengrin at your service, sir," a young voice announced as he opened the door. "My lord, I brought Star."

"Welcome, Sister Esther." Gyula ignored Dietrich and bowed to the young lady. "Were you able to rest well? You must be tired after what happened today."

The silent young girl wore a bluish-purple evening dress with violet brocade designs. Her red hair and white face were beautiful, but she seemed fatigued.

Esther twiddled with the rosary hanging from her neck as if that was her only hope.

Meanwhile, Gyula offered her a seat in the most businesslike manner. "Please have a seat, lady. This place was reserved for you," Gyula offered. "Please have supper with me. Dietrich, a job well done. Take a seat, as well."

"Thank you." Dietrich bowed and pulled out the chair for Esther.

Esther just stood there, so Dietrich placed his hand on the small of her back and whispered, "Why are you still upset, Esther? Sit."

Esther glared at Dietrich with cold eyes as she clumsily sat down. Two robots pushed out carts of food. They placed several hot dishes in front of the two Terran.

"Where is Father Nightroad?" Esther asked, as one of the robots filled the glasses with red wine. She totally ignored Dietrich and asked again, "Where is Father Nightroad? And where are my comrades? Where are they?"

"Your friends are all right," Gyula generously replied, not sharing the directions he had given to Radcon moments earlier. He didn't want to ruin their banquet with bad news. He raised his wineglass.

"Cheers. Please eat all you want. You're at the age when Terran eat the most, right?" Gyula said.

"You are finished, Marquis," Esther coldly stated, not looking at the tasty lamb soup in front of her. "Although the people tolerated your control of the city, you went too far this time. You burned down the church and killed the bishop. The Vatican won't let you get away with that!"

"Absolutely. Their military already has crossed our borders. City Military Police have been defeated left and right. They probably plan to take this city by tomorrow evening," Gyula answered.

Esther blinked in confusion after hearing Gyula's rather calm reply. *Why is this vampire so calm when the Vatican is slowly closing in on him? And the Vatican probably wasn't told about the deaths of the bishop and her clergy. Is the Vatican attacking, even though they assume the vampire has hostages?*

"How pitiful—they have abandoned you and your people," Dietrich softly added, placing his hand on the back of her neck. "All the Vatican wanted was a justifiable reason to attack this city. They didn't want to save your lives. Don't you get it?"

"Don't touch me, you filthy animal!" Esther snapped back, swatting away Dietrich's hand. "You jerk! You betrayed us and teamed up with a vampire. You should be ashamed of yourself!" Esther sternly said.

"Vampire, huh?" Gyula snickered at the conversation. He was smiling, but his eyes were dark and evil. The term "vampire" was one of the most troubling words between the two species.

"Vampire, bloodsucker, monster, haunted devils. Your kind calls us by those names. But why are you here?" Gyula asked.

"Eh?" Esther blinked.

"Why are you here?" Gyula gently repeated his question. But despite his tender expression, the question itself was completely cruel. "The reason you're here is because of that priest and Dietrich. Both of them betrayed you. The Vatican has forsaken this city and is trying to abandon the church. Were there any Methuselah, or what you call vampires, in that group of people?"

"Well . . ." Esther tried to argue, but couldn't.

Humans had betrayed her. . . . The Vatican had abandoned the bishop and her clergy. . . . She tried to find a convincing argument, but she couldn't.

"Forget it. That's your problem, anyway. Besides, seeing as you're not eating much, we should have some entertainment. Dietrich, prepare that item we discussed," Gyula ordered.

"Yes, sir," Dietrich replied. He chuckled at the silent girl, and then he snapped his fingers. The room instantly brightened and a dark curtain floated down.

This was a great chance to escape, but Esther just sat there with her mouth open. A large hologram appeared at the center of the table.

"What is this?" Esther wondered at the image of a dark blue area with random dark blotches scattered everywhere. She saw one white, cottony shape and realized that this was some sort of aerial map. But since the cloud was so small, the image had to cover an incredibly vast area.

"Hm, it's hard to see anything at this size," Gyula remarked.

Dietrich responded by reaching his hand under the edge of the table. A small keyboard slid out. Dietrich typed swiftly, like he was playing a piano concerto, and the image changed rapidly.

The map zoomed in on the central area. Esther realized that it was not a photo image, because the cars and clouds were still moving. This was a live feed.

"This is one-hundred twenty-five miles west of here. What you see there is the Vatican Eastern Army Sixth Brigade and Istavan City Military Police in battle," Dietrich explained while he manipulated the image.

Countless tanks and armored vehicles moved over the plains. The small dots appeared to be soldiers running. The two forces clashed in a struggle to take the hill.

"At this rate, the Vatican probably will come to Istavan by tomorrow. Gosh, they're so swift," Dietrich commented.

"They probably planned this a long time ago." Gyula chuckled at Esther, who was frozen in shock. He smiled out of confidence rather than evil intent.

Gyula asked, "Dietrich, where is the Star currently located?"

"Forty-four point five degrees north latitude, thirty-three point three degrees east longitude, currently above the territory of the Babylon Empire. We have been fully charged as of forty seconds ago. We are set in position to bomb for the next seven-thousand seconds," Dietrich replied.

"Oh, Sister Esther, we weren't talking about you," Gyula clarified. He was referring not to Esther as Star, but rather, something else also called *the* Star.

"The Star of Sorrow?" Esther asked.

"Yes, the Star of Sorrow. The ace up my sleeve." Gyula smiled gently. "Watch closely. This will be the final night for Rome, the capital that you Terran revere."

Istavan City Military Police were too slow, even when retreating, so Major General Humbert Barbarigo ordered his frontline assault units to slow down their pursuit.

"'We came, we saw, we conquered,' huh?" the middle-aged general quoted Caesar.

The area looked like a jumbled mess. At the far end of the plains, enemy soldiers were running for their lives. Grenadiers lobbed grenades toward them, as indicated by the grenades lighting bluish-white trails of light in the darkness. At the command post established at one end of the captured corners of the plains, dead enemy soldiers and piles of documents were strewn about.

For about an hour, the Vatican's Eastern Army Sixth Brigade, Justinians, led by Barbarigo, had dominated this battle. The skill level, motivation, and equipment of City Military Police paled in comparison to the Sixth Brigade. This fight was almost over before the Vatican used any of their mechanized units.

Even the military researchers were disappointed at the short battle, because they missed the opportunity to gather data on the effectiveness of their new weapons. "There is nothing but dust and ashes. We came here for nothing."

Major Marc' Antonio Vlaski's cyborg body made a grumbling sound, like it was complaining. His Gold Horn Knights, the Twenty-Sixth Mechanized Infantry Battalion, never joined the battle. The cyborg soldiers, mechanized thanks to lost technology, weren't able to take part.

"We can invade the Istavan castle tomorrow. Once your unit enters the city, you'll own the fight. Make your mark tomorrow," Barbarigo remarked.

"Sounds good. But, are you sure, sir?" the cyborg major asked, lifting one of his mechanical eyebrows. His metal eyeballs reflected the dark blue sky. "Once we enter the city, we can't avoid losing civilian lives. Also, we heard that the bishop and her clergy were held hostage there."

"Don't worry about the citizens. It's their own fault if they're still on the battlefield," Barbarigo replied. The military already had been authorized to conduct urban operations. Losing up to twenty percent of the citizens' lives was allowed. Priests—prepared to conduct mass funerals—already were on their way.

"Major, this is a holy war to kill vampires—mankind's nemesis. Shall we get down to business? I don't want Borghese to beat us there," Barbarigo said while he waved over his aide and chief of staff.

The Justinians attacked from the west, but Major General Borghese's Fifth Brigade, the Constantinus, attacked from the south. The enemy in the south wasn't too strong, so the Fifth Brigade probably was done with the initial battle and was prepared to move forward. Barbarigo didn't care about the City Military Police's toy soldiers, but he didn't want other friendly units to take all the glory.

"There might be enemy units left in the vicinity. Shall we request the aerial patrol ship *Sandolphon* to scan the area, sir?" asked Vlaski.

"I don't care. Just obliterate them. They can't stop us." Barbarigo blew off the chief of staff's question. "Hmph. Even if God himself appeared, they couldn't stop us."

"Hm?" Vlaski turned his head and looked toward the south skies.

"What's wrong, Major? Did you see an angel or something?" Barbarigo asked.

"Something peculiar on my radar. There's an ion flux somewhere in the sky," Vlaski replied.

"Ion flux?" Barbarigo asked, perplexed.

"This is strange. It's like . . . No, it can't be," Vlaski analyzed.

"Major, explain to us in layman's terms," Barbarigo requested.

"Sir, over there!" Vlaski responded.

Barbarigo turned around and gulped. All the other men also gulped at the incredible sight. The second moon was shining in the black sky. Unlike the first moon, which was always in the sky year-round, day and night, the second moon followed a twenty-nine-day cycle, going through different phases. But tonight, the second moon was glowing brighter than ever before. A large curtain of lights separated the moons and the earth.

"Why an aurora now?" Barbarigo sounded surprised.

The curtain of lights had a bluish-white glow. Normally, negative and positive ions from space caused friction with the upper skies and created an aurora at the North and South Poles only, so why was an aurora created here?

Is this a sign from God? Barbarigo thought. *Or are all these dead souls rising to heaven?* Barbarigo made the sign of the cross, just in case.

"What is that magnetic storm?!" Vlaski exclaimed. "Sir, a high voltage energy reaction—it's coming from above!"

Everyone looked up. The night sky burned and ripped apart, down to the ground.

✝

Reports came in, one after another:

"The Constantinus and City Military Police Third Regiment have been destroyed. The Justinians currently are searching and destroying City Military Police Second Regiment."

"The mayor of Istavan's satellite city, Carotia, announced a neutral position. They have requested the Vatican to deploy security forces."

"The air battleship *Nasargiel* deleted its original bombing missions. . . . currently analyzing battle damages."

Countless lighted dots on the map seemed to be moving around randomly.

Upon closer inspection, it was obvious who was about to win the war.

The Battle of Istavan, named by the Cardinals' Council, was about to end after only one day.

"We expect Istavan to fall by tomorrow," Francesco commented, his face illuminated by the hologram.

Caterina, standing next to her half brother, supported him by saying, "The war will probably end seventy-two hours after the declaration of war. Outstanding results, brother."

Francesco and the military leaders had executed their mission with splendid command and leadership. At the start of the war, an armored infantry company made up of mechanized soldiers and armored suits destroyed Istavan's City Military Police communications facilities. When the confused police tried to react to the ambushes, the Eastern Army's Fifth and Sixth Brigades—the Vatican's strongest forces—attacked from the west and south simultaneously. In reality, Istavan's overall strength paled in comparison to the Vatican military. With their main lines of communication disrupted, there was no way Istavan could claim victory. Currently, the Fifth and Sixth Brigades were advancing rapidly, destroying everything in their paths.

It's very impressive, Caterina thought.

Francesco had prepared his military for this battle; he had superior military prowess, a quality not usually found among the nobles or commoners. Though he was one of the prior Pope's illegitimate children, he easily could have ruled a kingdom or two with his military leadership alone.

"I'm aiming for total victory, Caterina," Francesco calmly stated, sounding humble yet confident. His saberlike eyes were sharp as ever as he continued to speak carefully. "It's written in the Bible, 'The Lord will gather warriors and soldiers to express his wrath toward those who don't follow His way.' Whether the nobles and common people—or even the Empire—defy God, His doctrine will be protected by force. In other words, when the doctrine is threatened, it is dangerous *not* to unleash the Lord's steel fists. As the representatives of Almighty God, we cannot ignore challenges to His authority."

Her half brother was correct, in a sense.

But . . . Caterina thought. She narrowed her razorlike eyes. Something bothered her. *Why did Istavan declare a war that they couldn't win? And the Star of Sorrow—when is the marquis' ultimate weapon going to be utilized?*

"Your Excellency, a message from the air battleship supporting the Sixth Brigade," reported a subordinate.

"Let's hear it," Francesco said.

The operator's report and Francesco's response interrupted Caterina's thoughts.

"This is Captain Arnold di Cambio of *Sandolphon*. We are ready to send you images of the ground forces, Your Excellency," the captain reported over the screen.

"Good job, Captain. I want visual confirmation of the situation. Send the image," Francesco ordered.

"Aye aye, sir!" The captain saluted.

A blue window appeared next to the captain. It was almost daybreak. Smoke rose from the ground in several places. At the top of the image, the armored units were pursuing City Military Police soldiers.

The captain provided details: "The Sixth Brigade currently is advancing west. As you can see, the enemy forces do not have enough power to counterattack. The brigade is on track to enter the city by tomorrow as they sweep and clear enemy forces along the way."

"I see. Regardless, stay alert. The marquis is still in reserve. Don't let your guard down until you destroy that vampire," Francesco warned.

"Roger that, Your Ex—" the captain was about to salute, but the image went fuzzy due to signal interference. The operator tried to adjust the image by reaching for the controls, but . . .

The ground was flooded with white light. All of the cardinals in the Dark Saint's Room shielded their eyes from the brightness. The next moment, the image went black. It happened in an instant, but it caused Caterina and the other cardinals to momentarily lose their vision.

"Wh-what just happened?!" Francesco bellowed as he violently rubbed his eyes.

The operators also were rubbing their eyes and babbling something, but they didn't seem to grasp what was going on. The operators grabbed the controls in confusion. One yelled out, "Your Excellency!"

The screen was still black, but Cambio's screams came through.

"What happened, Captain?!" Francesco yelled. "The screen is still black! What was that flash of light?"

"I-I don't know, sir. All of our fiber optics capabilities are inoperable," the captain's shaky voice reported. "But, we think . . . Oh Lord! What in the world happened?!"

"Captain, calm down and report to me! What is happening there?!" Caterina jumped into the conversation, sensing that something else might have gone horribly wrong. She ignored Francesco's condemning stare. *Is this possibly their weapon?*

"This is a direct order from a cardinal. Captain Cambio, report what happened as quickly and as accurately as possible!" Caterina ordered.

"S-something happened down on the ground," the captain's voice quivered. Captain Cambio articulated as well as he could. "The Sixth Brigade and the City Military Police unit that they were pursuing have been obliterated! Obliterated is an understatement: There is nothing left on the ground!"

After being shocked into silence for a long while after the white twister disappeared, Esther finally uttered, "Ah."

In the hologram, the plains were burnt to a crisp. Thousands of soldiers and the latest weapons were reduced to ashes and dust. The plains were ominously quiet.

Everything had died. They were gone.

"This is the Star of Sorrow, the ace up my sleeve," Gyula said with satisfaction.

The Star of Sorrow, a mobile, electric-laser-firing satellite, was a conglomeration of lost technologies. It orbited a low path above Earth at a rate of thirteen-thousand feet per second, and it emitted a laser energy pulse twenty-two times per second. The energy pulse was eight-hundred gigajoules, the power of two-hundred tons of TNT. It could obliterate Rome with five pulses.

Esther didn't blink as she stared at the hologram. Her shoulders didn't stop shaking until she spoke. "Why?"

"Hm?" Gyula responded to Esther's whisper.

Esther looked up with teary eyes and repeated her question, "Why do you do such things? Killing the bishop, her clergy, and the townspeople—that wasn't enough for you? Why do you want to murder so many people? Do you like to kill that much?"

"I don't like to kill. I don't have poor taste," Gyula answered.

"Th-then *why?* Why do you do it?!" Esther demanded.

"To live. I do it to survive," Gyula responded.

"Live?" Esther choked at his response. She looked at the vampire in confusion.

Gyula continued, "Yes, I do it to survive. Tell me, Esther, why do you fight me? Why do you and the other Partisans try to kill me?

"Well, because there were no other options," Esther replied. Why was she conversing with a vampire? "You and your men have continued to kill many innocent humans. The city was ruined, many children died of hunger, and many older people froze to death. I couldn't abandon them. I know that no matter how bad a person is, it's still sinful to kill someone. But I couldn't abandon these people. In order for us to survive, we . . ." Esther stopped in mid-sentence and gasped.

"Seems like you found the answer." Gyula let out a sad laugh; then he stood up. The sky started to get brighter. Gyula opened the windows of the balcony and looked back at the girl. "Let's say that Methuselah were caught by Terran—say, the Vatican. We would be tortured with silver needles and wooden stakes, so we'd beg for our lives: 'Please stop' or maybe something along the lines of 'don't hurt my wife and children.' But would the Terran stop? No. And, in reality, that would be righteous," Gyula remarked.

"B–but, even so!" Esther blurted.

Gyula continued, "Listen, Sister Esther. Don't cover your ears or close your eyes. This is a fight for survival. Us versus them: Methuselah and Terran, vampires and humans. This is merely a battle for survival of the fittest. There can be only one winner and one loser. There is no such fantasy as coexistence. I know that." Gyula paused, calmly looking at the shivering girl. He then turned to Dietrich and ordered, "Prepare for the next shot. The target is forty-one point fifty-three degrees north latitude, twelve point twenty-nine degrees east longitude—Central Rome."

"Roger. It'll take ten minutes to recharge," the handsome Terran boy answered without emotion.

Gyula lightly nodded; then he turned to Esther and said, "Oh, that's right, Sister—I need to tell you something. I lied to you about one thing."

Gyula felt that he should be merciful; but on the other hand, he thought it would be unfair if he held back information from this gentle but courageous young girl.

It was strange for a Methuselah to apply fairness when dealing with a Terran girl; but nonetheless, he expressed a shocking statement, "The Partisans and that priest—your friends that were captured this morning—are no longer alive. They were executed."

II

kay, get off!" a voice barked. A figure pushed Abel out of the car. The sky was pitch black.

The city lights were far away and flickered in the cold air. Both Abel's shoulders were hastily wrapped with bandages, and his knees could give out any minute from the gunshot wounds.

He barely managed to stand up and look around. *Is this an airport?* Abel wondered as he took in a runway and a simple, concrete control tower. At the far end were surveillance biplanes, and a military airship circled about in the double-moon sky.

Istavan didn't have any civilian airports, so this must have been a military airport—pretty far from Buda. *But why were we transported here?* Abel wondered.

"Hey, fancy meeting you again, Father," a gruff voice called out from afar.

Abel turned around to see a fish-faced giant walking toward him from the control tower. Behind the man, City Military Police prodded about a hundred men and women. All had chains on their hands and feet, and their clothes were tattered. Most were seriously injured.

"All right, Partisans, get on the other side of this line! Father!" Radcon ordered the captured people to get on the runway's previously drawn line. He was waving around the same crossbow that Esther had used.

"We'll have an abbreviated court session. I'm the judge. I'm also the prosecuting team. And you have no defense lawyers," Radcon announced.

The Partisans must have been beaten repeatedly, because most of them dropped to their knees from exhaustion, unable to talk back. In their place, Abel spoke out with a weak voice, "If this is a court session, then what are we charged with?"

"You all are charged on multiple counts of murder, robbery, arson, and the betrayal of Istavan. The judgment is . . . the death penalty!" Radcon declared.

A few soldiers laughed, whistled, and made lewd comments at the Partisans' predicament. The Partisans lost all hope and moaned.

"We'd like to go slowly, killing you guys like we did the bishop's group; unfortunately, we don't have the time. Instead, you will be executed by that thing," Radcon pointed his chin to the black airship in the sky. Underneath its large balloon, a line of huge machine guns pointed downward. Radcon waved his arms, and the bridge responded by flashing a searchlight several times.

"That is our military's pride—air battleship *Charkane*. The airship will conduct an air-to-ground attack exercise, and you'll be the targets. Of course, you can run around all you want, but don't come onto this side of the white runway line. If you do, *we'll* shoot you," Radcon explained.

Radcon's deep-set eyes glinted with an evil joy. He toyed with the crossbow and sneered. "Please entertain us, Father, just like the other group did."

"Colonel, did you really kill the bishop and her clergy?" Abel asked.

"Tsk. It was fun. We cut off the men's arms and legs, feeding those limbs to the dogs. We raped the sisters, and then we sliced them up. They were snobby—but they were only women, after all. Vitez was the best-tasting one yet. What a babe. She was raped by at least thirty men several times over. It was great." Radcon cackled.

Abel bit into his lip until it went white. He looked down, suppressing his anger.

Radcon truly enjoyed the sight of Abel's shoulders shaking. "We wanted to play with you, as well, but we're too busy for that. We hope you don't feel left out," Radcon stated.

"Have you not begun yet, Colonel?" an emotionless voice asked from behind.

The giant frowned as he turned around and asked, "What are you doing here, Major Iqus?"

"Patrolling. I finished checking the status of the air defense units as Lord Gyula ordered, so I decided to watch the execution," Tres answered in a matter-of-fact way. He walked rhythmically toward the giant, his collar flapping in the wind. He didn't seem to feel the cold at all. "The orders for execution were authorized more than an hour ago. What is cause of the delay?" Tres inquired.

"Shut up; we've got nothing to do anyway. Let us have some fun, at least." Radcon pouted, upset like a bulldog that had his bone taken away. "Okay already, let's waste them! Tell the *Charkane* to do their thing!"

One of the soldiers hastily turned on the radio that was strapped to his back. He yelled into the handset and the airship responded by turning on its engine.

"Hey, start running, Partisans! It won't be much of an exercise with all of you clumped together!" Radcon growled, and he pulled the trigger of the crossbow. The thick arrow stabbed into Abel's lower leg.

The airship lowered its altitude and pointed its Gatling guns toward the ground. The guns' eerie movements prompted the Partisans to get to their feet and run for their lives.

"Ha! Run, you maggots!" Radcon's laugh was muffled by the roaring automatic fire. The rounds kicked up dirt on impact, the bullets trailing right behind the fleeing Partisans.

"Ha! The *Charkane* is playing with them." Radcon sneered at the airship. The Partisans didn't have enough energy left to be nice—they began to push, shove, and step on one another to dodge the bullets. The Gatling guns aimed for the back end of the group.

"Don't give up. Please get up, Ignatz!" The tall priest bolstered the fat man's shoulder to help him up. Ignatz had been shot in the leg, so they'd wound up at the end of the group, their legs tangled every which way.

Radcon peered through his binoculars and ordered his subordinate, "Tell them to take good aim at the priest."

The Gatling guns roared again, this time digging a dirt trail straight toward Abel.

"Got him!" Radcon yelled.

The other soldiers hooted when the dust covered the two men. Suddenly, the area became bright.

"Wh-what?!" The soldiers looked up and saw a huge ball of light. By the time they realized the *Charkane* was on fire, a second artillery round pierced through the helium balloon and struck the gondola.

"Th-the *Charkane!*" a soldier yelled. The airship split in half and burst into flames. The ball of fire slowly floated to the ground, slammed into a hill next to the runway, and burst into fiery pieces.

"What happened?! Who did it? Oh, look!" Radcon scanned the sky and couldn't believe what his enhanced eyes saw. "An air battleship?"

A white, virginal shape dropped in altitude at an amazing speed. It appeared to be a huge airship with graceful curves and an elegance to it. But the white body had bloody red lettering: *Arcanum Cella Ex Dono Dei,* Latin for Papal State Affairs Special Operations Section.

"V-Vatican! It's a Vatican air battleship!" Radcon exclaimed.

A female voice spoke through the static. "This is the Vatican AX air battleship, *Iron Maiden II*. I am Sister Kate, the captain of this ship. This is a warning for Istavan City Military Police. As of now, I have taken over this airport by force. Throw down your weapons and surrender. I say again, throw down your weapons!"

The pleasant voice announced unpleasant news. Gunfire proved that the threat wasn't empty. The shots illuminated the sky with ruby-red trails, hitting the biplanes along the runway and cutting them to shreds.

"Wh-what's the air defense artillery doing?!" Radcon hollered. *Why didn't their radar detect such a large ship?!*

Radcon grabbed the collar of a soldier who was carrying a radio. He yelled into the handset, "Air defense unit, what are you doing? Hurry up and shoot down this monster!"

"It's no use, Colonel," Tres interrupted in a cold voice. "They have been destroyed. There are no survivors," Tres explained.

"Quit lying, Iqus! The air defense unit is waiting right over—" Radcon stopped in mid-sentence. He pointed with his crossbow at the tall tubes behind the control tower, but what he saw confirmed what Tres had said before.

"I checked on the status of the air defense units."

"Major Iqus, d-don't tell me you . . . ?" Radcon stuttered. "Partisans! Take the Partisans hostage!" he yelled to his troops.

The soldiers, realizing that they had no place to hide, decided to use human shields. A soldier reached for the tall priest, grabbing his silvery blond hair. "Come with me, priest! You're my hostage."

The soldier suddenly became silent. Blood was spurting everywhere. He crouched in confusion and uttered, "Ah?" When he noticed a fist-sized hole gaping through his chest, he already was falling down on top of the other dead bodies.

"Weren't you told to surrender?" Iqus asked as he wielded two large handguns. Tres had just killed his own soldiers without passion.

"Major Iqus, why you . . . !" Radcon scoffed.

Tres remarked, "Forty-four hundredths of a second too late." He moved his gun but not his eyes.

Before Radcon could pull the trigger of his crossbow, Tres had shot a round into Radcon's guts.

"Rewriting combat mode to genocide mode. Combat open," Tres announced in a cold manner as he shot down four soldiers. Blood spurted from their chests. They fell. A soldier tried to shoot Tres with a machine gun, but his arm was shot off instantly.

"Major Iqus! Are you betraying us?" Radcon bellowed.

"Negative. I was never part of your group," Tres replied.

"What?! Then why were you . . . ?!" Radcon yelled. He was interrupted as he watched a round pierce through a soldier's mouth before it came out the back of the man's head. The headless corpse fell forward.

"I suggest you surrender." Tres dropped empty clips from his guns as he explained, "All of you are guilty of attacking the Saint Mathias Church. We will have you make statements at San Angelo Castle. You will be taken alive."

"San Angelo Castle. So you're a Vatican pawn!" Radcon growled.

"Watch out, Tres!" Abel exclaimed.

Radcon leapt at Tres from behind. He held a dead soldier's mechanized hand, which had withstood a thirteen-millimeter gunshot and still gripped a machine gun. Radcon was right behind Tres, who had no rounds left in his handguns.

"Die, Iqus!" Radcon yelled as he fired at Tres with multiple rounds.

Tres turned around and was hit with multiple streams of bullets, which shredded his long coat.

"Ha ha! Go to hell, you traitor!" Radcon laughed as soon as he finished firing all the automatic rounds.

He kept laughing at the cloud of gun smoke and smell of gunpowder that surrounded Tres.

Radcon boasted, "I will not be killed by a stupid Vatican pawn!"

"Negative. Colonel Radcon, I don't intend to kill you. I will take you to Rome alive," an ice-cold voice announced through the gun smoke.

Radcon couldn't believe his eyes. The coat and ground had enough holes that they resembled Swiss cheese.

Tres' coat was torn to shreds, but Tres just stood there with his arms crossed, as if nothing had happened.

"N-no way," Radcon gulped. "He's not human."

"Not human? Affirmative. I am not a human," Tres replied. He opened up his arms and revealed that he hadn't shed a single drop of blood.

Through some parts of the torn clothing, the artificial, shape-memory, plastic-alloy muscles had several blunted bullets stuck to the surface.

The young officer—or rather, Killing Doll—introduced himself with a mechanical voice, "I am AX Agent HC-IIIX—Hercules Tres Iqus—code name Gunslinger. And I am not a man. I am a machine."

"Dammit!" Radcon bellowed as he rushed Tres. The ground shook from his heavy mechanical footsteps. "Die, you Doll bastard!"

"Twenty-five hundredths of a second too late," Tres said calmly as Radcon's boulderlike fist swung toward his face. With a slight flick, he slipped out new clips, dodged Radcon's punch by lightly jumping to the side, loaded the clips into his guns, and aimed his M13 pistols at Radcon.

Radcon was shot eight times. He spurted blood.

Radcon had been shot in the elbows, shoulders, knees, and hip joints. Even an enhanced mechanized soldier could not stand up if shot at those weak points. He crumbled to the ground, broken. "Y-you purposely—"

"I told you. I am taking you alive, Colonel Radcon," announced Tres. His glass eyes glinted coldly. "You will not die here. We will prepare an interrogation room at San Angelo Castle for you. We want a complete confession from you. It's obvious that you won't die from these minor wounds."

Tres ignored the giant and turned to Abel, who was crumpled on the ground.

"Clear. Damage report, Father Nightroad," Tres requested.

"So you finally moved. You're late, Tres," Abel chastised the warrior. "I was wondering when you'd come out for some action."

"Negative. You just deviated from your schedule. I executed my moves on time according to the original plan," Tres responded.

"On time? Then . . . ?" Abel asked.

"Unfortunately, two hundred seconds ago, we confirmed the first attack by the Star of Sorrow," Sister Kate announced through Abel's ear cuffs. "We have new orders from Cardinal Caterina. Father Tres, take the city with the help of the Partisans. Father Abel, ride my airship and stop the Star of Sorrow, no matter what."

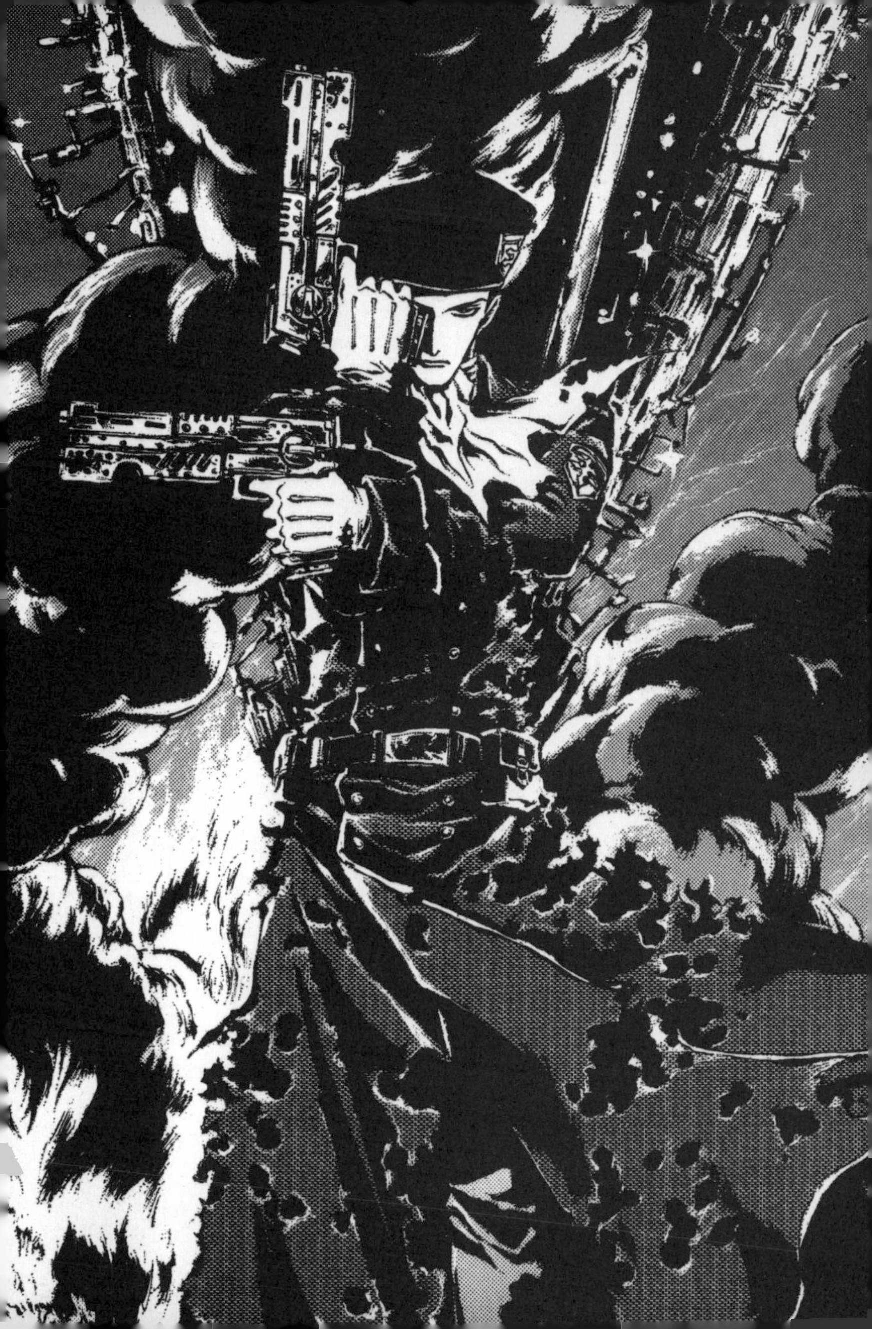

III

A dull sound coming from afar shook the anti-UV glass windows. The cold soup, which had never been tasted, rippled at the sound waves. Gyula turned around. "What happened?"

"Something occurred at the airport." Dietrich grabbed his coat just as a red pillar of fire shot up from the airport. "I'll go check it out and return shortly."

Esther saw Dietrich sprint out of the room. Gyula's statements still rang through her head.

The Partisans and that priest are no longer alive. Esther had no one left. No one. *What should I do?* she thought. It didn't seem real at all. She pushed those thoughts aside. Instead, Esther focused on trying to figure out how to stop the vampire.

She no longer had any comrades, and she was up against a vampire. Even a hundred soldiers probably couldn't defeat this horribly strong monster. So it was something a little girl wouldn't dare do.

But she had to do it.

Stop blaming yourself and focus on what you need to do—that's what the priest said. Esther knew she had to defeat Gyula. She needed to avenge the deaths of her friends and prevent him from taking the world away from humans.

But how? How can I defeat this monster?

Esther subconsciously grasped the rosary. She stopped. The rosary was made of silver and had a sharp edge. If she stabbed him in a vulnerable area . . .

For vampires, silver was almost as fatal as ultraviolet rays. Though they could withstand gunshots and stab wounds by normal metal, their body reacted differently with silver. Any wound caused by silver could be fatal for them.

But vampires were extremely swift. Even without using their haste mode, they had superior reflexes and strength in comparison with humans. Gyula easily could snap her neck with a flick of his wrist.

She needed to find a way to get closer to him.

Esther stood up. "Wh-what a beautiful woman," she complimented, indicating the painting on the wall. She tried to suppress her tremors as she walked toward the painting. She hid the rosary in her hand. "She's very beautiful. Is she related to you, Marquis?"

"She was my wife." He, too, approached the painting now. "She was the last person I lived with. She was wonderful." The vampire practically pressed his face to the painting, his back to Esther. "She's no longer here." His voice shook slightly. "She died. She was . . . killed by her own kind," Gyula remarked.

"Eh?" Esther stopped in her tracks. "What do you mean? Killed by her own kind?"

"Maria was a Terran. She was a Terran like you. But because she loved me, the church rejected her. And one night, they gathered the townspeople together and they all killed her!" Gyula punched the wall. His nails bit into his palms until he bled. "Why? Why exactly do humans despise us so much? I would understand if they killed *me,* but why did they kill my innocent wife—one of their own?!"

The beautiful woman in the painting smiled sadly at her husband. It was a magnificent portrait, and it was hard to imagine that the subject had been gone for more than ten years. This painting only made Gyula sadder.

He continued, "I wanted to seek revenge—not just on the townspeople, but all the Terran and the Vatican. I wanted to kill all of them with the relic their ancestors and my wife left behind!"

"Relic? What relic?" Esther asked.

"The Star of Sorrow. My wife fixed the control system of the Star. I met her when I hired her as a programmer to revive the Star," Gyula explained.

Of all the lost technology from before the Armageddon, computers were the most mysterious items. Only highly skilled programmers could decipher the overwhelming lines of numeric codes.

"The Star isn't the weapon you think it is. After the Armageddon, this satellite was used as a relay point by our ancestors to channel energy. The solar power generators on the moon emitted energy microwaves that the satellite picked up; then they sent as a laser down to Earth for energy consumption. If it were fixed properly, this poor town and all the other developing towns might have been revived. But the church mistakenly thought my wife and I were creating a weapon of mass destruction, so they killed her," Gyula stated.

The concepts Gyula explained were beyond Esther's comprehension, but one thing was clear: This vampire, at one time, actually had made efforts to redevelop her city. It was hard to believe that this monster that had terrorized the townspeople actually had tried to help humans before!

"After my wife's death, I couldn't revive the relic by myself. Then, an organization called the Orden approached me and offered to send a programmer to help. This organization had both Methuselah and Terran members, but I had no idea who these people were. They did mention that they were against the Vatican," Gyula continued.

"That was good enough for me. They helped me resurrect the Star of Sorrow by sending Dietrich, a programmer and a member of the Orden," Gyula explained.

Esther gripped the rosary with her sweaty hand and tried not to give into her confusion. This vampire sought revenge for his wife's death and went against the Vatican, whereas Esther sought revenge for her family's deaths and wished to kill the vampire. Was there any difference between the two?

"Everything was for vengeance. That's what you said, right, Marquis?" Esther confirmed.

"Yes. I challenged the Terran to avenge my wife's death. I wanted to kill them," Gyula responded.

Then this was Esther's way of seeking revenge, too.

Esther raised her rosary. Gyula was deeply preoccupied, so he left his back vulnerable. Esther raised both her arms, lifting the rosary like a knife. If she swung down toward his neck, the vampire would die.

She held her breath and brought the rosary down toward his neck.

"But now that I think of it, I might have been wrong," Gyula commented.

Esther's hands stopped for a moment. If she had swung all the way down, the rosary would have stabbed him. But Gyula's comment, mixed with sorrow and regret, made Esther hesitate for just a moment. It was a fatal mistake.

Gyula turned around by chance. He saw the sharp shiny object in Esther's hands and his eyes filled with rage.

"Haaa!" Esther finally swung down, but she had lost her balance. There was no way she could stab accurately from such an unstable position.

Gyula grabbed the rosary with his hand, breaking the skin on his palm just by a few millimeters. It emitted an odious smoke. "Why, you Terran!"

Gyula swung his arm and flung Esther into the air.

She slammed into the wall and bounced onto the floor. She coughed at the strong impact. Esther tried to catch her breath, but Gyula grabbed her hair.

"Terran!" Gyula held her up, her feet dangling. He bared his fangs. He no longer wore the gentle look from moments before; He had turned back into the world's most fearful creature of the night—a vampire.

"How dare you trick me into getting attacked, you dirty monkey! You mocked my tender memories!" Gyula scowled.

He grabbed the writhing girl's chin with his wiry fingers. Her veins pulsed on her neck. Gyula growled and aimed his fangs at her throat.

At that moment, the anti-UV glass windows cracked open.

"Esther!" Abel cried out. He shot Gyula's shoulder . . . just before the marquis' fangs pierced Esther's neck.

IV

The silver bullet knocked the vampire to the ground. Abel ignored him and went straight toward Esther. As she gasped for breath, the priest pulled her up by her shoulders.

"Are you okay, Esther?" Abel asked.

"Ah, Father." Esther squinted at Abel. "So you *are* alive."

"Yes. I'll explain later. Right now, we need to get out of here!" Abel said.

"N-no! We need to stop the Star, or else Rome will be destroyed!" Esther cried.

"Rome? What do you mean?" Abel asked.

"It's—F-Father, behind you!" Esther shrieked, her eyes wide open.

Abel didn't turn around. Instead, he rolled to the side with Esther still in his arms. But something slashed at his priest robe.

TWANG!

The shining object adjusted and came toward them again. Abel kept rolling. By the time he stood against the wall, his robe was torn to pieces, and blood trickled from deep cuts.

"No way!" Abel sighed. If he hadn't had on glasses, his eyes would've been poked out. "No way! I shot him with a lot of silver bullets!"

"Damn Terran," Gyula scoffed in rage. From his fist, a bony blade protruded. His suit was full of bullet holes—blackish-red liquid oozed out. The wounds were black at the opening, indicating a reaction to silver, which was fatally poisonous for a Methuselah.

The vampire, not feeling any pain, dug into his wounds with his blade.

Esther, looking at the horrendous sight, gasped, "Eek!"

Gyula dug out the silver bullets from his flesh, also removing chunks of his poisoned skin. Only after he flung off blackened bits of flesh from his blade did he show signs of pain.

"Abel Nightroad, you Vatican pawn! Very good timing. I was just about to destroy Rome," Gyula announced. He raised his other arm. Another blade protruded from that hand. "Unfortunately, you won't be alive to see the destruction!" Gyula clanged the two blades together, causing an unpleasant, high-pitched sound.

Right as Abel scrunched up his face at the awful noise . . .

"Shaah!" Gyula jumped and punched out his blades in rapid succession.

Abel pulled out his gun just as quickly. The sounds of the hammer cocking and the trigger squeezing echoed almost simultaneously.

Gyula didn't even bother dodging the six rounds. He stabbed the air where Abel and Esther used to be and sank into the wall. His bony blades were made of microfolds and could vibrate at high speeds. The natural, ultrasonic blades created a horrible vibration riddled the walls with holes.

"Amazing dodges. No wonder you're an AX agent. Are you an enhanced human?" Gyula commented.

Abel took a step back as Gyula approached him.

None of Abel's shots hit Gyula. The ultrasonic blades had vibrated the rounds into dust.

TWANG.

Gyula crossed the blades like a crucifix and smiled eerily. "What's wrong, Crusnik? I thought you were going to kill me and stop the Star of Sorrow. It'll launch in less than a hundred seconds, you know?"

On the table, a small holographic timer counted down.

"Target location, forty-one point fifty-three degrees north latitude, twelve point twenty-nine degrees east longitude. Central Rome bombing in less than ninety seconds," a mechanical voice announced.

"If you're not moving, then I'll come to you!" Gyula blurted.

Abel hesitated to point his gun at Gyula, who was closing in on him. *These bullets won't take him down. What next?*

"How about this?!" Abel threw a metal flask full of gunpowder at Gyula. He shot the flask in midair. It exploded into flames. A wall of fire stood between Abel and Gyula.

"Did I get him?!" Abel wondered.

"Kaaaah!" Gyula placed his blades together and used them to shield himself as he ran through the blaze.

"What?!" By the time Abel realized that the vampire had cut through the fire using ultrasonic vibrations, it was too late. He was pushed back by a ball of white light.

"Urg!" He somehow was able to push Esther aside before he slammed against the wall. His left arm was crushed so badly that he could no longer feel it. His glasses were shattered by the ultrasonic waves.

But the scream didn't come from Abel.

"Gaaaah!" Gyula grabbed his right arm, where the blood spurted out from his missing forearm.

As they crossed each other, Abel had shot multiple rounds, blowing off Gyula's arm. Now the vampire couldn't use one of his ultrasonic blades anymore.

Abel didn't feel superior; rather, he sympathized with the suffering Methuselah. He aimed right between the marquis' eyes and squeezed the trigger.

Gyula groaned as red blood gushed from him. Foam flowed from his purple lips. He dropped to his knees. "O-oh God. No!"

"F-Father!" Esther saw the priest fall instead of Gyula.

The priest's last round had shot the portrait of Gyula's wife right between her eyes. Gyula's right forearm—the one that had been shot off—had stabbed through Abel's stomach. Using his left arm, Gyula had grabbed the blade and pierced the priest's body from behind.

"Father! Father!" Esther screamed.

Gyula watched Esther running toward the priest and remarked, "It's over." The digital counter was down to fewer than ten seconds.

Seven seconds.

Abel coughed up blood. He surely would die.

Five seconds.

The eerie aurora draped across the sky. The Star was gathering energy.

This satellite was supposed to make people happy. It was supposed to make Gyula and his wife happy.

One second.

"Done." Gyula sighed.

The next moment, there was an explosion.

V

There was a bright flash and a deafening explosion. All the anti-UV glass windows shattered, fragments scattering into the center court.

"Wh-what happened?!" Gyula yelled as he swatted away glass shards. His body felt almost weightless after the impact. It was hard to see the area in the whiteout. His eyes were forced shut from the sudden changes in pressure and light. Even a Methuselah would take several seconds to recover vision after such a bright flash. When Gyula finally could see, he gulped.

"P-Pest!" Gyula stuttered. A large portion of the city was obliterated and had been replaced by a huge crater. The water from the Danube River had changed course and started to pour into the new crater.

Gyula knew what caused the explosion. "The Star of Sorrow!" It was the only weapon capable of such destruction. *But it was supposed to be aimed at Rome, not here! Why?*

"No! It was aiming at the wrong target!" Gyula looked at the numbers on the control panel, checked the status of the satellite and target coordinates, and so on. The coordinates were different from what Gyula had directed, though. And, on top of that, the Star already was recharging for yet another target!

"No way! It's not possible. Dietrich! Someone, get Dietrich!" Gyula hollered.

"Did you call, Marquis of Hungary?" A hologram image appeared on the table.

"Dietrich, where in the world are you?! Come back now!" Gyula demanded. "The coordinates are wrong! If you don't adjust them, Istavan will—"

"The coordinates are wrong? No, sir. The coordinates are very accurate." Dietrich smiled, predicting Gyula's anger. *"The second shot is aimed at City Military Police headquarters. The third shot will aim at the center of Pest. And the fourth shot will hit the Valley of Blood, your palace. My program is perfect."*

"What are you saying? D-don't tell me, you . . . ?!" Gyula stood there, forgetting the pain from his arm, enraged. "Dietrich! You betrayed me! You used me."

"I didn't use you. I used the Star of Sorrow. What value is one stupid monster, anyway? Don't overestimate yourself."

"Wh-what is your objective?!" Gyula bellowed at the sight of the angelic smile on Dietrich's face. "You promised to help me get revenge. Were you lying about helping me fight the Vatican?!"

"I didn't lie. Fighting the Vatican is one of our goals, but our objective isn't as crude as your avenging your wife's death. Our vision is a lot larger than you can imagine. Don't measure us with your small ruler," Dietrich mocked Gyula.

Gyula pondered at Dietrich's statements. He blurted, "I get it! You guys weren't aiming to destroy the Vatican in the first place! You wanted to use the Star of Sorrow to instigate a war between the Vatican and the Empire, right?!"

"Oh, great deduction. You're correct." Dietrich complimented Gyula like he was a child. *"As you said, we wanted the Vatican to start a war with the Empire. That is the Orden's wish."*

The Vatican and the Empire haven't had any large-scale conflicts for several hundred years. Of course, there were small fights here and there. For example, two-hundred and seventy years ago, the Eleventh Crusade of Pope Sylvestor XIX waged a holy war that ended in utter defeat at Debrecen, one-hundred twenty-five miles east of Istavan. But no major conflicts had happened since then.

There were several reasons for not waging war, but one of the biggest reasons was the city of Istavan, located between both factions. The humans considered this a free city, whereas the Methuselah recognized it as sovereign territory of the Marquis of Hungary. The city was in a unique situation. It acted as buffer between the two groups. If one of the groups were ever to invade this city . . .

"We wanted the two groups dragged into war. But we don't want Rome to perish. We want the Vatican to crush the Empire," Dietrich explained.

"What? What is the Orden?!" Gyula howled. "Answer me! What is the Orden thinking?! What is the point of pitting the humans against vampires?! Which side are you on?"

"We're not on anyone's side. We are Contra Mundi, the Enemy of the World," Dietrich replied.

"Contra Mundi?" Esther furrowed her brows. She couldn't understand half what Dietrich was saying, but it sounded so sinister all the same.

Contra Mundi—it was the perfect name for the devil with an angelic smile.

Dietrich enjoyed watching Gyula gnash his teeth, but he glanced at the fallen sister near the wall. *"Hi, Esther. Isn't this unfortunate for you? I actually fancied you, you know."*

"Shut up, jerk!" Esther glared back. "You are the worst! How many times do you need to betray people?"

"I didn't betray anyone because I wanted to. But I suppose I must have upset you quite a bit." Dietrich pushed back his bangs away from his face. His light brown eyes gazed at Esther as he said, *"Then let me teach you something. Listen carefully. Memorize this magic spell: 'Igne Natura Renovatur Integra. With our fire, we will renew the world.'"*

Abel, wrapped in Esther's arms, jerked at Dietrich's phrase.

Esther didn't notice. She asked, "Huh? What's that?"

"It's the self-destruct code for the Star of Sorrow. I kept this code a secret from the marquis. If you type this phrase on the keyboard, the Star will self-destruct," Dietrich explained.

Esther sensed Gyula's shock at the knowledge that such a code existed.

"Liar! I won't fall for that!" Esther yelled.

"You hurt my feelings. I shared that with you as a way to apologize to you." Dietrich sadly sighed. *"Just try it, anyway. You'll understand my true feelings then."* He glanced to the side deliberately. *"That's if you can type in the code without interference, of course."*

Gyula and Esther glared at each other like rival gladiators; then they simultaneously turned to look at the keyboard.

"Goodbye, Esther. I love you. And good luck." Dietrich chuckled.

As soon as his hologram disappeared, they both dashed to the keyboard.

"I need to stop it!" Esther cried.

"No!" Gyula spouted.

Esther was closer to the keyboard.

"I won't let you!" Gyula called out.

The vampire's speed outpaced hers. Gyula pushed Esther to the side and covered the keyboard with his body. "The Star of Sorrow is my last hope! I won't let anyone destroy it!"

Esther sat up and touched a cold metal object on the floor. "Don't be ridiculous, Marquis!" she snapped. "You heard the traitor, right? If you don't do anything, you'll die!"

"We don't know that! If I can adjust the controls . . ." Gyula said.

"We don't have enough time!" Esther grabbed the object and lifted it. It was heavier than she imagined. She cocked the hammer. "Please get out of the way! Let me destroy the Star!"

"I should have killed you, Terran," Gyula said, looking at Esther with disgust. A blade protruded out of his hand again. "Either way, I have to kill anyone who knows the self-destruct code. Die!" Gyula jumped on her.

Esther squeezed the trigger impulsively, and then she cocked the gun again. She squeezed once more—but she realized her mistake.

The gun was empty!

"Die, Terran!" Gyula thrust his blade toward the girl's neck. Esther shut her eyes and assumed that her head would be sliced off with one stab.

Instead, she heard two bodies collide with a *thud*.

"Y-you!" Esther heard Gyula's voice stutter in confusion. "What? How can a human move with those injuries?"

Esther didn't know what was going on. She opened her eyes cautiously and saw a figure, wearing a priest's robe, standing in front of her.

VI

Gyula was alarmed: The injured priest now stood between him and the nun.

Abel was battered from head to toe. His bandages were dripping with blood, and Gyula's right arm still was stuck in his stomach, the blade pierced through his back. Most humans would have died from with those injuries.

But though the priest's face was flushed, he didn't seem to be in any pain. He didn't seem angry, either. His winter-blue eyes were full of sorrow.

"Father, you're not human, are you?" Gyula pushed down with his blade.

Abel caught it between his hands.

Gyula gritted his teeth. Only a few things, like a bear, could match the powerful strength of vampires, but the priest was holding his own. *Is the priest an enhanced human, a mechanized robot, or . . . ?*

"Aaaauuuughh!" Gyula tried to kick the side of the priest's head. Terran reflexes would be too slow to dodge a vampire's swift and heavy kick. If the priest were human, his head would have been ripped from the neck to spurt a fountain of blood.

But instead, Gyula was flung away. He curled up into a ball and hit the wall with his feet, bending at the knees to absorb the impact. After landing on the ground, he stammered, "Wh-what? Why are you so strong?!"

"Have you ever thought about this?" the priest calmly began. He pulled out Gyula's severed arm from his stomach and continued, "Humans eat cows and chickens. Vampires drink the blood of humans. So maybe there is something that drinks a vampire's blood to live."

Gyula couldn't believe what he was seeing. Fangs protruded from the priest's mouth. In the next moment, his fangs bit into Gyula's severed forearm. Blood trickled out the corner of Abel's mouth as he drank from the arm.

"N-no way . . . Blood . . . He's drinking my bl-blood?!" Gyula stuttered.

Gyula's right arm shriveled. Abel sucked all the blood from it, leaving behind only skin and bones.

What in the world is he?! Gyula thought. He stepped back. His teeth chattered. The priest wasn't a Terran nor a Methuselah. *Is he an enhanced human? A cyborg soldier? No, not any of those.*

A low, grumbling voice said, "Nanomachine 'Crusnik 02' forty-percent limited performance—authorized." The priest's winter-blue eyes turned blood red. He dropped the shriveled arm on the ground and said, "I am a Crusnik—a vampire that drinks the blood of vampires."

"I've heard about you." Gyula bit his own lip so hard that he cut himself. "A special section of the Vatican has a monster that it uses to conduct unusual, covert missions. So you're that monster!"

"Gyula Kadar, Marquis of Hungary, in the name of the Father, the Son, and the Holy Spirit, you are under arrest on charges of murder and disturbing the peace. Drop your weapons and surrender," Abel warned.

"Over my dead body, Vatican dog!" Gyula growled, and his single blade vibrated and split into three separate blades. The three blades vibrated, creating ultrasonic waves, heating up the room. "I am the Marquis of Hungary! A highly noble Methuselah! I refuse

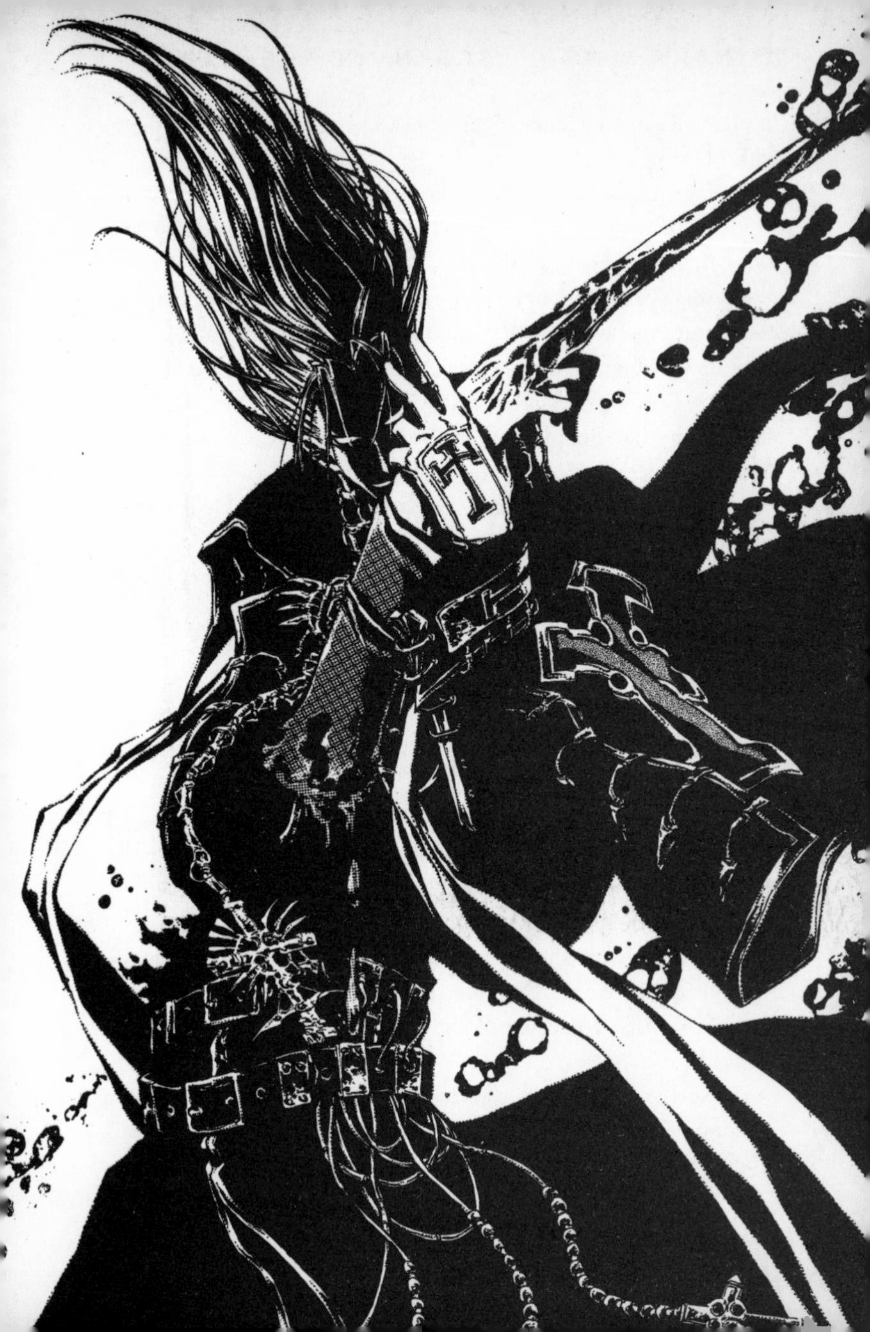

to surrender to a Crusnik or any Vatican pawn!" Gyula stood there with his arms raised.

Abel jumped up to the ceiling, but Gyula ran up the walls after him. "I've got you!" He stood upside down on the ceiling and swung his triple blade at Abel. "Die, AX Agent!"

Abel's arm split open. Instead of red blood, a black liquid oozed out. Abel gripped the wound, which gleamed eerily, as if it were metal. Huge scythes expanded from both ends of his arm.

Abel's scythe clanged with Gyula's blades, screeching like nails on a chalkboard would. "Lord Gyula, please surrender," Abel suggested.

The AX agent possessed overwhelming strength. He slammed Gyula to the floor below.

The red-eyed monster landed softly and stood next to the vampire. He emphasized kindly, "I don't want to hurt you any more."

"Shut up! I am the Marquis of Hungary! I will not bow down to a Vatican pawn!" The nobleman still refused. He pulled back his left arm. "No matter what happens to me, I will take you down with me, Nightroad!"

His triple blade vibrated. Gyula once again rushed toward Abel. He swung, but Abel dodged. Gyula's blades bit into the wall. Shards of plaster scattered. Gyula withdrew his arm.

Abel swung his scythe at Gyula but missed.

Gyula kicked the ground and thrust his blades out while he flipped forward. His weapon got caught in Abel's scythe, but Gyula used that resistance to flip sideways and strike again with his blade.

Abel slid backward, clashing his scythe with Gyula's blades, creating sparks. The two tangled together, rolling toward the wall. Abel was cornered.

Gyula pushed his blades against Abel's scythe and laughed. "You're done, Nightroad!"

Gyula's eight ribs extended out of his body like sinewy white snakes. They attacked Abel from all sides. Abel's hands were occupied holding back Gyula's blades, so there was no way he could dodge the rib spears.

"What?!" Gyula winced when his rib spears were diverted. Something had unleashed and wrapped around Abel's body. Hard as diamonds, it pushed away the rib spears.

"Wings. You have *wings,*" Gyula remarked. Behind Abel's waving, silver hair, a huge shadow moved. Large black wings began to spread.

"What *is* a Crusnik?!" Gyula yelled.

"I am a Crusnik," Abel responded.

Gyula's eyes opened wider as he stammered, "No! Then you're . . . N-no, you—"

Abel's black, sharp-edged wings completely spread out and started flapping. They muffled Gyula's yells. The black wings snapped Gyula's blades.

Without any weapons, Gyula was powerless against Abel's scythe.

"This is the end," Abel announced. One black wing swung down on Gyula.

VII

Did you kill him?" Esther asked.

The priest didn't reply. Though his black wings and scythe had retracted and disappeared, his eyes still glowed blood red.

"Father, what are you?" Esther asked.

"Esther, you need to worry more about yourself than about me," Abel responded.

He put his glasses into his chest pocket and looked at Esther. "Please take care of that."

In the hologram, the countdown still continued. An aurora was beginning to form again. Esther thought to say something, but she ran toward the keyboard instead.

Abel looked down at his feet. In the pool of blood was the nobleman, his right arm cut off at the shoulder and a deep slash in his stomach. But he was a Methuselah and had superior vitality.

"Why don't you kill me?" Gyula asked in a hoarse voice. "Your mission was to kill me. Are you trying to torture me?"

"My mission was to destroy your Star of Sorrow, not to kill you, Marquis. And I don't torture people for fun," Abel replied.

"People?" Gyula repeated. He looked at Abel, confused.

Is this priest calling a vampire like me a person?

"Yes, you are a person. Esther, how are you doing?" Abel quietly asked.

"Well, I finished typing it in. I learned how to type on a typewriter when I assisted the bishop with her work, but I've never used a keyboard before," Esther answered. She confirmed what she had typed on the screen.

Igne Natura Renovatur Integra.

Esther double-checked the phrase she'd never heard before, and then she pressed the enter key. "This should do it . . . Eh?!" Esther's brows furrowed.

The countdown continued.

"I wonder what's wrong with this thing." Esther continued to press the enter key, but nothing changed. The Star of Sorrow should have self-destructed by now. *So why is it still counting down?*

"What is going on?!" Esther exclaimed.

"What's wrong?" Abel stood next to Esther and stared at the screen. His brows also furrowed. "That's funny. Did you enter the code correctly?"

"Yes, just as Dietrich said," Esther responded.

"Hi, Esther." The screen switched from the image of the controls to the handsome devil with that angelic smile. *"If you're looking at this screen, that means that you typed in the code I suggested."*

"D-Dietrich!" Esther barked. "Wh-what are you trying to do?!"

"Esther, calm down. This isn't a live feed. It's a video file," Abel pointed out. The image in the screen continued to talk.

"Esther, I need to apologize about something. The code that I asked you to input wasn't for the Star to self-destruct. It was only a code to change the target coordinates."

Esther's face went pale.

"Don't worry. Istavan is no longer in danger, because the new target is now Byzantium. Oh, do you know where Byzantium is? It's the capital of the Empire, a nest full of despicable vampires," Dietrich clarified.

Esther did notice that the coordinates had changed. She didn't know exactly where the new coordinates pointed, but if they really were aimed at the Empire . . .

"If the Empire is attacked with this, then they surely will retaliate. The humans and vampires will start another war. How does it feel, Esther, to know that you pulled the trigger that will start a war?" Dietrich asked.

"Y-you jerk!" Esther spouted, even though she knew it was only a prerecorded image of Dietrich. "A jerk to the very end!"

"You're so naïve to keep believing a person who keeps fooling you. Well, I did like that part of you, too. Goodbye, Esther. Hope to see you again." Dietrich chuckled as his image disappeared.

Esther continued to glare at the screen.

A bloody hand reached for the keyboard.

"Father!" Esther exclaimed.

"Esther, please step aside." Abel gently nudged aside Esther and stood in front of the keyboard. The color of his eyes had returned to normal. He looked down at the screen.

"It's no use, Father Nightroad," Gyula commented. "The Star of Sorrow is a special computer. If Dietrich told the truth, then this relic existed long before Armageddon. There's no way you can—"

Abel ignored Gyula's comments. He silently stared at the massive amount of numbers on the screen; then he started typing. He typed slowly at first; but gradually, he picked up speed.

"Um, Father?" Esther said. She stared at the amazing sight. Abel was typing at an alarming rate, as if he were playing the piano. Programming required special skills and knowledge, so a novice like him probably couldn't do much.

"F-Father, don't type numbers randomly," Esther remarked.

"Please be quiet," Abel requested.

Abel continued to type furiously, as if he himself had turned into a machine. All the while, the countdown continued.

Abel tried to beat the clock by typing rapidly, but the machine announced, "Forty seconds until bombing. Thirty-nine, thirty-eight, thirty-seven . . ."

Abel heard the countdown and stopped typing.

He raised his face, ignored Esther's worried looks, and stated calmly, "Program manager voice input. Switch to system administrator mode."

The machine stopped counting down and the numbers on the screen froze. It was as if the computer had stopped to listen to its old master's voice, like a pet dog perking its ears.

"Affirmative," a woman voice responded, sounding like a servant responding gently to her master. "Switching to system administrator mode. The current task will continue in this mode. Thirty-nine, thirty-eight, thirty-seven . . ."

"Sourcing system emergency operation command files. Freeze all other tasks," Abel ordered.

"System manager deleted the command files. Access error source R20055," the computer announced.

"Deny," Abel responded.

It sounded like the devil was speaking to God in a foreign tongue. Esther could only stare at Abel as he spoke in an unknown language.

"How many files can use the system freeze command? We don't have time. You don't need to display the address," Abel commanded.

"Affirmative. Begin search . . . complete. One file fits the inquiry," the computer responded.

"Which one?" Abel asked.

"Security regulation three zero nine zero, self-destruct code," the computer answered.

Abel hesitated. He glanced at Gyula, but there was no more time to waste. "Activate self-destruct code. Based on security regulation three zero nine zero, self-destruct."

"Code input requires authorization of Special Class A or above. Please state your authorization," the computer requested.

"My administrator authorization is . . ." Abel took a deep breath and responded, "UNASF Lieutenant Colonel Abel Nightroad. Red Mars Project Manager, Security Section. Authorization UNASF nine four dash eight dash RMOC dash six six six dash zero two AK," Abel answered.

"Authorization confirmed," the computer announced. "We will now initiate self-destruct based on security regulation three zero nine zero. Due to the self-destruct code, the seven seven eight two satellite will be destroyed."

Numbers on the screen disappeared, one line after another.

The priest continued to stare at the darkening screen. He sighed, and then he spoke softly to something beyond the windows. "Thank you for working for such a long time."

He looked up toward the moonlit sky. The first moon rose up from the east. The second moon hung permanently in the same point in the southern sky, as if it were an evil eye looking down on humans—which is why it had been nicknamed the Vampires' Moon.

Gradually, a small light near the second moon flickered and disappeared.

"Wh-what happened?" Esther whimpered. She had a very difficult time comprehending everything, but she knew something important had occurred.

"What happened? Where did the Star go?" Esther asked.

"The Star no longer exists," Gyula responded from the floor. "The Star doesn't exist anymore. It's over. Well, it was forced to end." Gyula looked at Esther with gentle eyes; then he glanced at the priest. "You are who I thought you were, Father Nightroad."

Abel shook his head. Whether he denied Gyula's statement or simply wanted the vampire to stop speaking was unclear.

But Gyula nodded anyway. Then he changed the subject. "By the way, can you do something for me, Father Nightroad?" Though his arm was cut off, he still was able to speak in a hoarse voice. "If I'm sent to Rome, I will be executed. If I'm going to die, I don't want Department of Inquisition killing me; so, can you give the sister a chance to act on her revenge?"

Esther was surprised. She looked at both Abel and Gyula.

Gyula looked at Esther's bloodied face and gently said, "I took the lives of people she cared about. She has a right to kill me. It's right and just. I should die at her hands."

Abel was at a loss for words. Eventually, he picked up his percussion revolver. "Esther, please take this," Abel said as he reloaded the pistol, cocked the hammer, and placed it in the nun's hand. "A silver-tipped bullet is loaded. If you shoot his heart, he will die instantly."

Esther hesitated to hold the heavy handgun. She looked down at the weapon and then to Gyula, who was lying in a pool of blood.

"I'm so sorry," Gyula apologized to the girl. "My revenge was right. I won't let anyone deny that. But I also took the lives of people you cared about, so you have a right to seek revenge."

"I . . ." Esther shook as she held the cold metal gun. The priest's warm hands wrapped around her own. *What should I do?* The bishop who raised her like her own child, her Partisan comrades, the townspeople . . . they all were killed by this vampire.

She did want to kill him. She wasn't God or an angel: She knew how to love, but she also knew how to hate.

And she realized that the man in front of her embraced those very same feelings. "I hate you. I want to avenge the deaths of the bishop and others; that's a fact." Esther slowly spoke. "But I think it's wrong to shoot you."

She looked at Gyula and shook her head. She finally glanced up at the priest with a lost expression and said, "I'm pretty stupid, but this doesn't make sense. I don't know, but I think somehow that this is wrong. Father, am I weird for thinking this way?"

"No, not at all." Abel smiled and shook his head. He said to Gyula, "Hatred doesn't create anything. Well, I shouldn't be the one saying this, but that's how it works, Lord Gyula. So, please don't force her to pull the trigger. . . . " He sighed. "Well, the city has finally settled down, hasn't it?"

There were occasional explosions and gunshots heard from the city, but it was gradually lessening. It was only a matter of time before the city would return to its normal state.

Abel waved at a new shadow entering the palace. "Hi, Tres. Is your mission complete?" Abel asked.

"Affirmative. We have subdued ninety-seven percent of City Military Police," Tres replied. The voice of AX Agent Gunslinger was as emotionless as usual, but his answers were extremely accurate and to the point. "After their headquarters were destroyed, most of them lost their will to fight and surrendered. Partisans and townspeople assisted, so the fighting was held to a minimum. Currently, the *Iron Maiden II* and some Partisans are sweeping the area to capture any remaining enemy soldiers. They will complete their task by the time we return to the Vatican," Tres reported.

"That's great," Abel commented. The town had been regained successfully without an urban battle. But the Vatican would have to take good care of Istavan during the redevelopment phase to avoid friction with the neighboring countries. The redevelopment would go at a rapid pace, repairing buildings, providing food, and so on. They needed to rebuild the city so the townspeople could survive the winter.

Abel looked at the balcony again. Voices indicated that a few Partisans approached the palace.

"Well, shall we go? We can leave the rest to the Partisans," Abel said.

"I'm not letting you go, you damn dogs!" the giant standing in the center garden growled. He wore a dark blue uniform, tattered and stained in blood and dirt. But his fish-face and gruff voice were unmistakable—it was Radcon. *How did he escape from the Partisans? It's amazing that he can still stand after being so violently battered.*

He was still holding Esther's crossbow. Now, he aimed it at her. "Die!"

Esther couldn't move.

Tres pulled out his M13 handguns and shot over his shoulder without looking back. The thirteen-millimeter round sliced right between Radcon's eyes and burst out the back of his head.

Radcon flew back on impact.

The arrow shot.

"Marquis!" Esther shrieked. Gyula was suddenly in front of her, with the silver nitrate-tipped arrow piercing his chest.

Gyula fell back. He smelled of burnt flesh.

Esther kneeled and brought him into her arms, but he already was convulsing. "Why? Why did you save me?" Esther asked.

"I don't know. . . ." Gyula replied. With a silver nitrate-tipped arrow piercing his heart, there was no way the Methuselah could survive. Gyula coughed up blood and foam, and his eyes slowly went white. "I hate the Terran. I have no idea why I saved one—and a novice, at that."

"Don't talk!" Esther embraced Gyula as he chuckled painfully. Esther couldn't save him; she could only look up to the two priests. One didn't express any emotion and the other was flabbergasted, shaking his head.

"Where did I go wrong? Why did I . . . ?" Gyula whispered. He looked up at Esther even though he couldn't see anymore. He was no longer in pain. He even looked peaceful. "All I wanted to see was your happy face, Maria. Why did it have to be like this?"

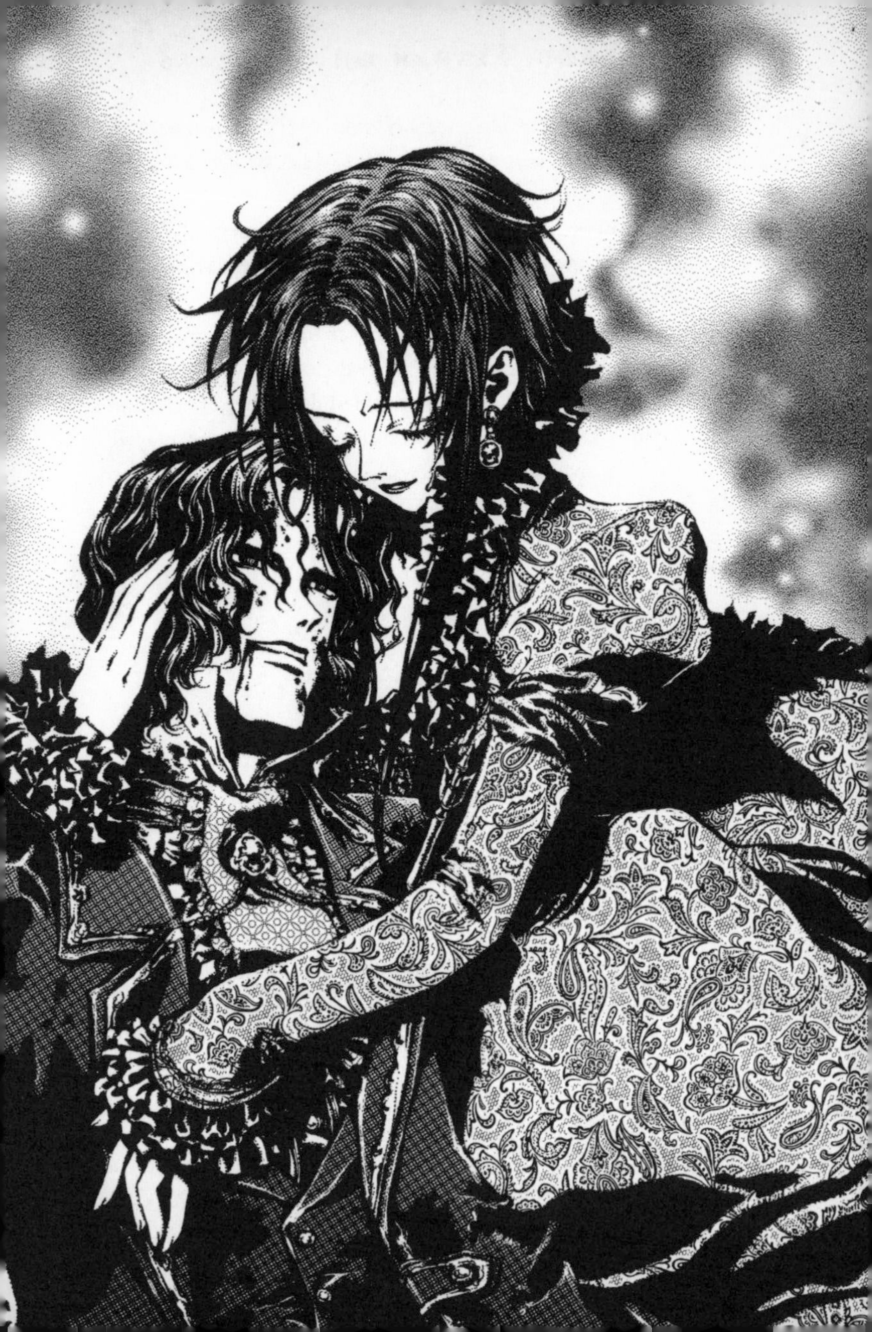

Esther knew he couldn't see her anymore; she also realized he was envisioning someone different. He was talking to someone else.

Esther brought her cheek close to his and whispered, "Thank you, dear." For some reason, she didn't feel weird saying that. "Thank you. You've done enough. Thank you so much."

Gyula smiled. His eyelids closed, never to open again.

"Oh Lord, may he rest in peace," Esther said.

Why am I crying? Esther's tears trickled down her cheeks and fell onto Gyula's face. She made the sign of the cross and prayed, "May he rise to heaven and reunite with his beloved wife, and then may he beg for the Lord's mercy. Amen."

EPILOGUE:
THE HUNTER'S AFTERNOON

For blood it defileth the land;
and the land cannot be cleansed
of blood that is shed therein, but
by the blood of him that shed it.
—Numbers 35:33

Spring came early in southern Europe.

This year, spring came *very* early. It was less than one week after the end of Carnival, but the air already was getting warm. Worshippers from various regions came to visit Rome, enjoying the warm spring air as they walked through Saint Peter Plaza.

"So, spring has come already," a beautiful woman in a cardinal's robe said with a sweet voice. She was looking down at the worshippers below.

Soft sunlight filtered into her well-organized office. Her health was not the best, so she welcomed the warm season.

The Vatican had been extremely busy, with employees working hard to assist in the redevelopment of Istavan after the recent battle. Even the Duchess of Milan, Cardinal Caterina Sforza, Minister of Papal State Affairs was kept busy with the redevelopment. She had coordinated the assistance of war victims, appeased upset nobles and commoners who had opposed the battle, and so on. Things finally had slowed down in the past few days.

"Well, I must get back to the reports," Caterina remarked as she left the window and sat. She placed her elbows on her desk, intertwined her fingers, and rested her chin on her hands. She looked at the priest standing at attention.

"In your reports, Dietrich von Lohengrin—a programmer who manipulated lost technology—was noted, but do you know where he may have gone? Any leads?"

"Negative," Tres answered tonelessly. The small priest wearing a neatly groomed robe continued his report, "Currently, we have no leads on his background, status, or whereabouts."

"I see," Caterina responded.

She had predicted that. If Dietrich was exactly as Abel had described in his report, he would be too clever to leave any clues behind, anyway. But, after causing such a large incident without leaving any evidence, one had to deduce that a larger organization was backing him.

"*Igne Natura Renovatur Integra* . . . so the Contra Mundi is still in business, I suppose," Caterina remarked. Her razorlike eyes sparkled behind her monocle.

If that organization was involved, then it would be extremely difficult to find more evidence, provided if they hadn't destroyed it already. They were extremely clever and cautious; Caterina knew this from her dealings with them in the past.

"We have a limited amount of AX Agents. This investigation has reached a dead end. Duchess of Milan, are there any other sections that can assist us in this matter?" Tres asked.

"Why do you ask?" Caterina tilted her head.

The Istavan incident was written off as a simple vampire case. The motive behind the Marquis of Hungary's actions to disrupt several hundred years of peace and boldly challenge the Vatican never was reported. The marquis was a vampire, an enemy of humans. Vampires were not assumed to possess human motives; no one in the Vatican would waste their time trying to fish for something that didn't exist.

He wasn't supposed to have a motive.

"I guess there is one exception to that." Caterina talked about someone else who came to her mind. The priest who considered vampires to be people currently was not in Rome. He still was executing a mission to take care of the city until things settled down.

"By the way, when is Father Nightroad coming back?" the beautiful cardinal asked as nonchalantly as possible.

✝

The morning snow froze into ice by afternoon.

A girl dusted snow off the gravestone and laid down a bouquet of winter roses. "Bishop, I wanted to tell you that I made the decision to leave."

The carving of the Holy Mother Mary didn't respond; it only smiled gently.

The church's backyard was full of new graves. The simple gravestones were spaced out evenly and lined up in an organized manner. Now, they were covered in light snow. The whole place seemed so holy.

It had been more than three months since the incident, but none of the townspeople came to the graveyard, probably because the tragic memories were still too real for them to bear.

"The town is lively again. Most of the injured have recovered. The new bishop and clergy offered to keep me here, but I have decided to go to Rome. Why did you and the others have to die? I think my job is to find out why," the girl continued.

She grasped the rosary hanging around her neck.

Why couldn't I save my family? She felt sick every time she asked herself that question. She sometimes woke up in the middle of the night, screaming.

"I need to focus on what I have to do next. I believe that's the best way to go," she said.

She looked across the graveyard. At the end of the row of graves was a small gravestone. There was no name or date written on that grave. She was the only person who knew who was buried there . . . along with a portrait. If the church found out that a non-human was buried there, her transfer orders to Rome surely would become orders for incarceration in the church penitentiary. Those who supported her as the Partisan leader would turn around and accuse her of being the equivalent of a witch.

Of course, what she did probably was not wrong. But the church called it a sin.

"I want to find out where you and the others came from. I'll decide to hate you or not after I've found answers," she remarked.

The girl stood up in front of the grave where Gyula and his wife rested. The train was going to depart soon. She picked up her suitcase, turned around, and walked to the station.

She stopped at the row of Italian cypress trees when she noticed a tall figure entering the graveyard. The man noticed her, too, and he smiled behind his glasses and a large bouquet of winter roses.

"Are you leaving now?" the tall priest asked.

"Yes. It's time for me to go," the girl answered.

The priest had nothing else to say. He let her pass through. The girl bowed lightly and walked away, stepping on fresh, white snow. She entered the horse-drawn carriage that waited for her at the front gate. Once the priest saw her get in, he turned and walked down the aisle of graves.

They didn't bother to look back at each other, because they knew they would meet again. . . .

In Rome.

To be continued . . .

EXTRAS

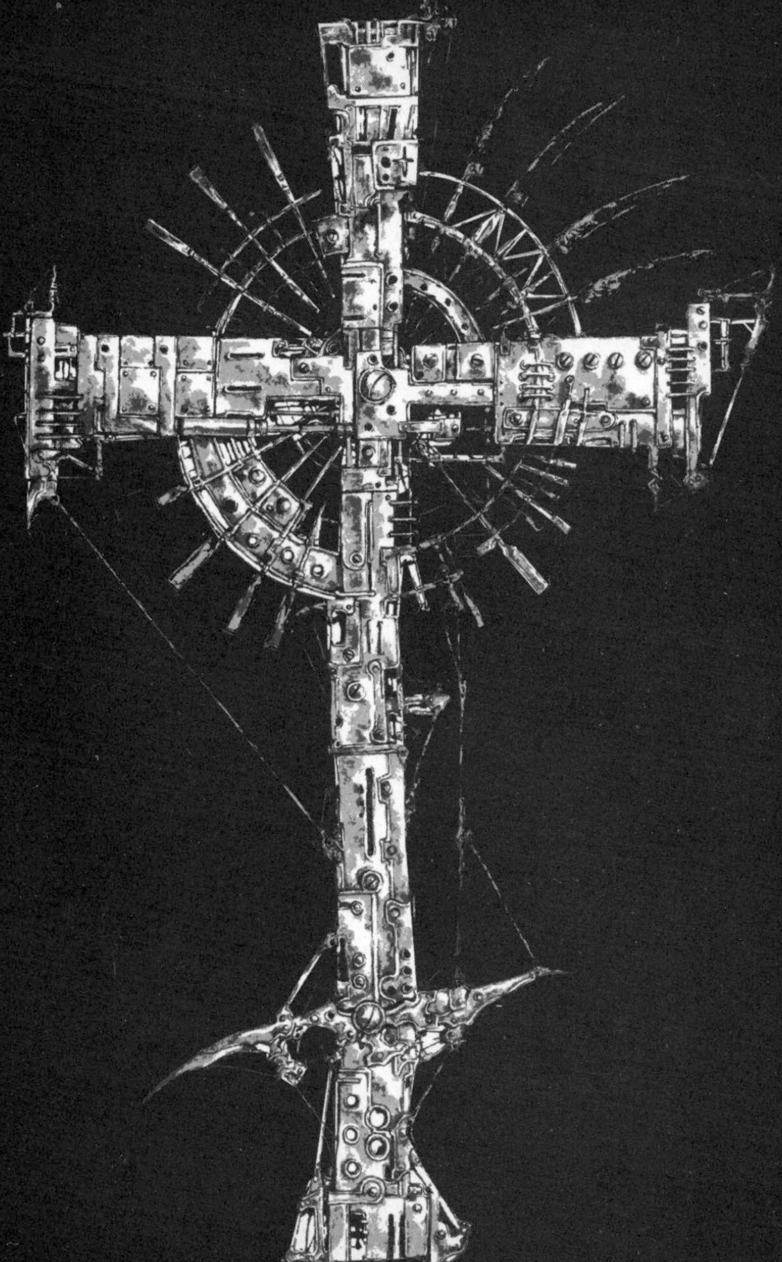

The World of Trinity Blood

Albion Kingdom

Four-City Alliance

Germanic

④

⑧

Kingdom of Franc

Vatican Territo

⑦

⑥ Carthenia Dukedom

Hispania Kingdom

⑤

Hispanic Territory of Morocco

City of Freedom Carthage Territory

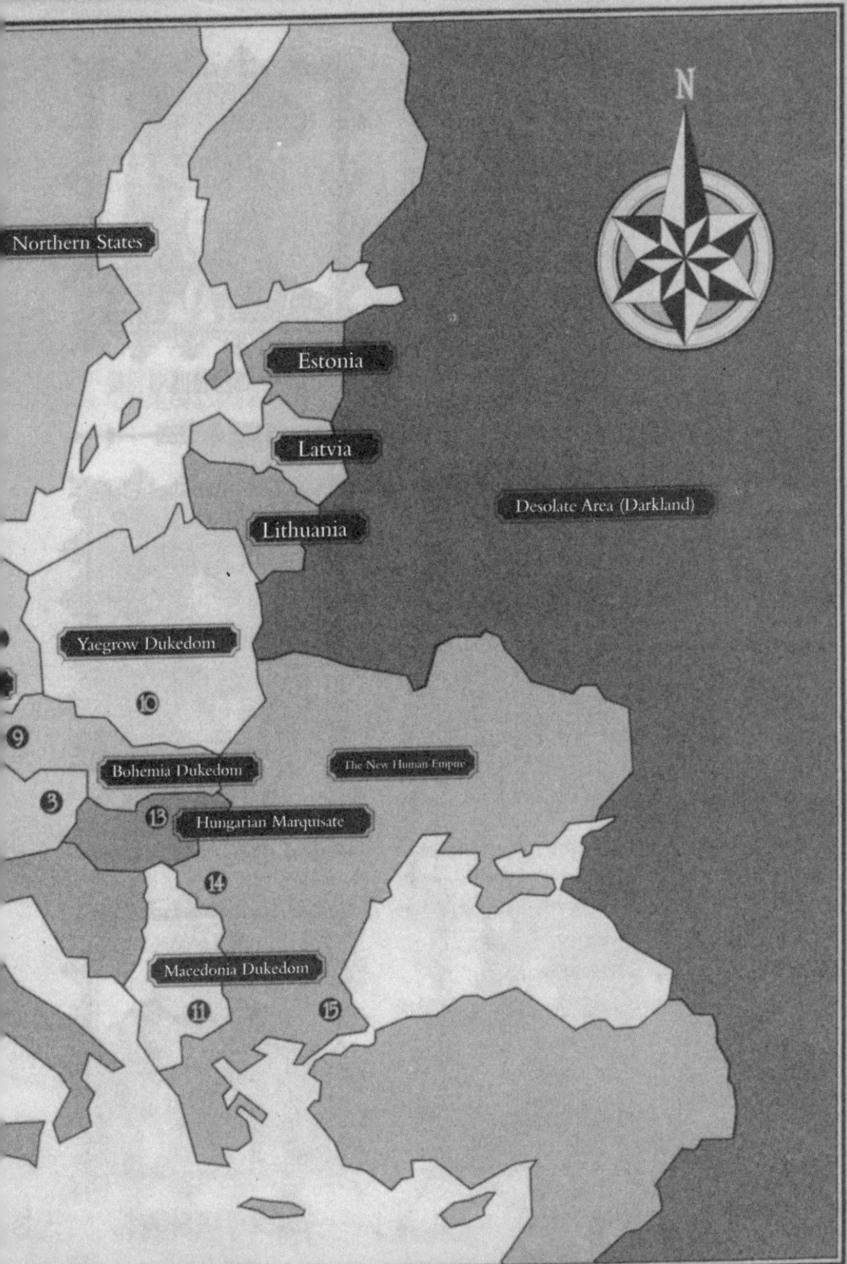
N
Northern States
Estonia
Latvia
Lithuania
Desolate Area (Darkland)
Yaegrow Dukedom
10
9
Bohemia Dukedom
The New Human Empire
3
13
Hungarian Marquisate
14
Macedonia Dukedom
11
15

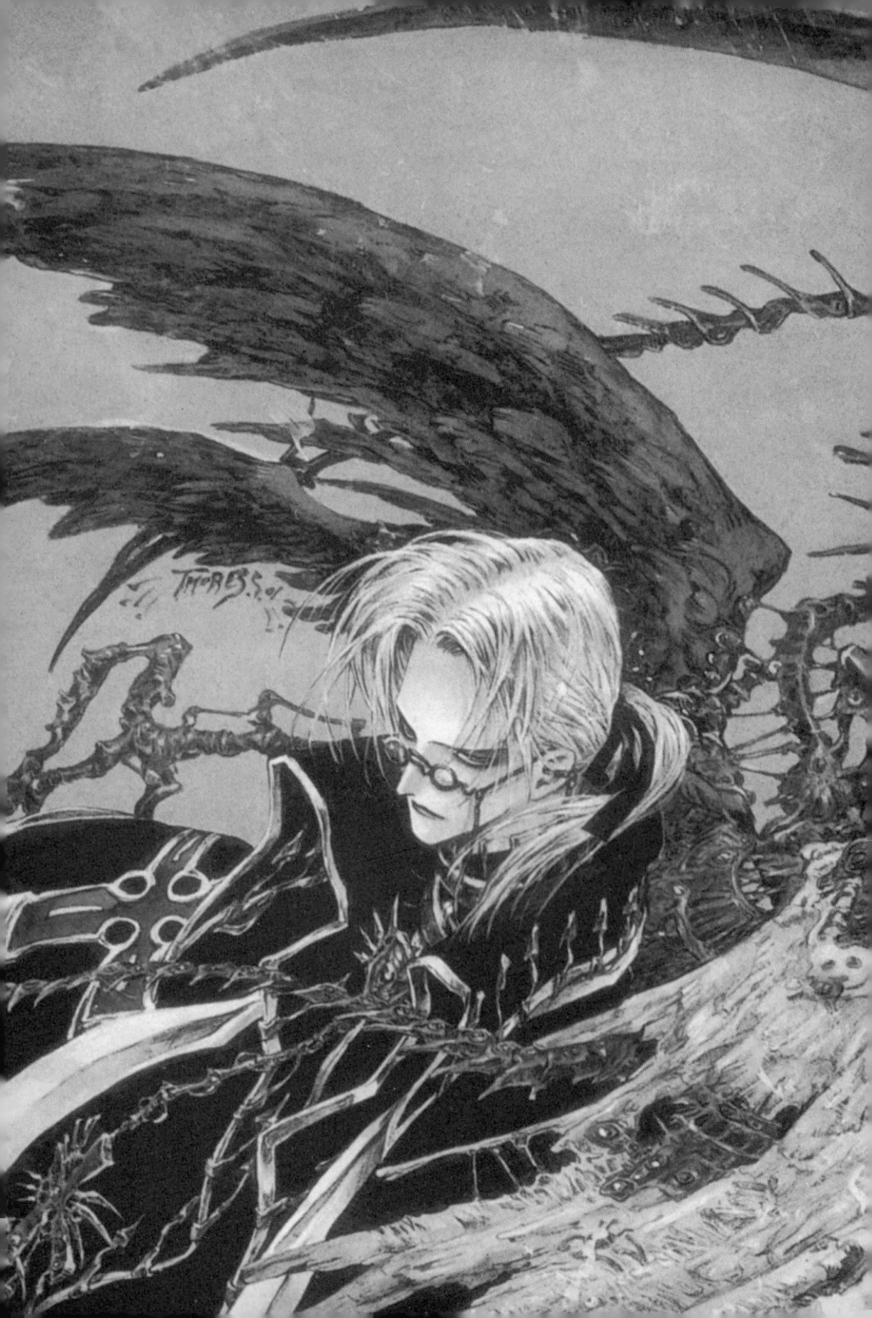

The condemned one,
bearing the cross of atonement.
The fallen angel, spreading
its black, lacquered wings.
He who holds the
sword of conviction . . .
Goes into the
dark night alone.

A single flower blooms in a frozen, ruined capital. What does she see through her blue eyes? A future full of hope, or just despair?

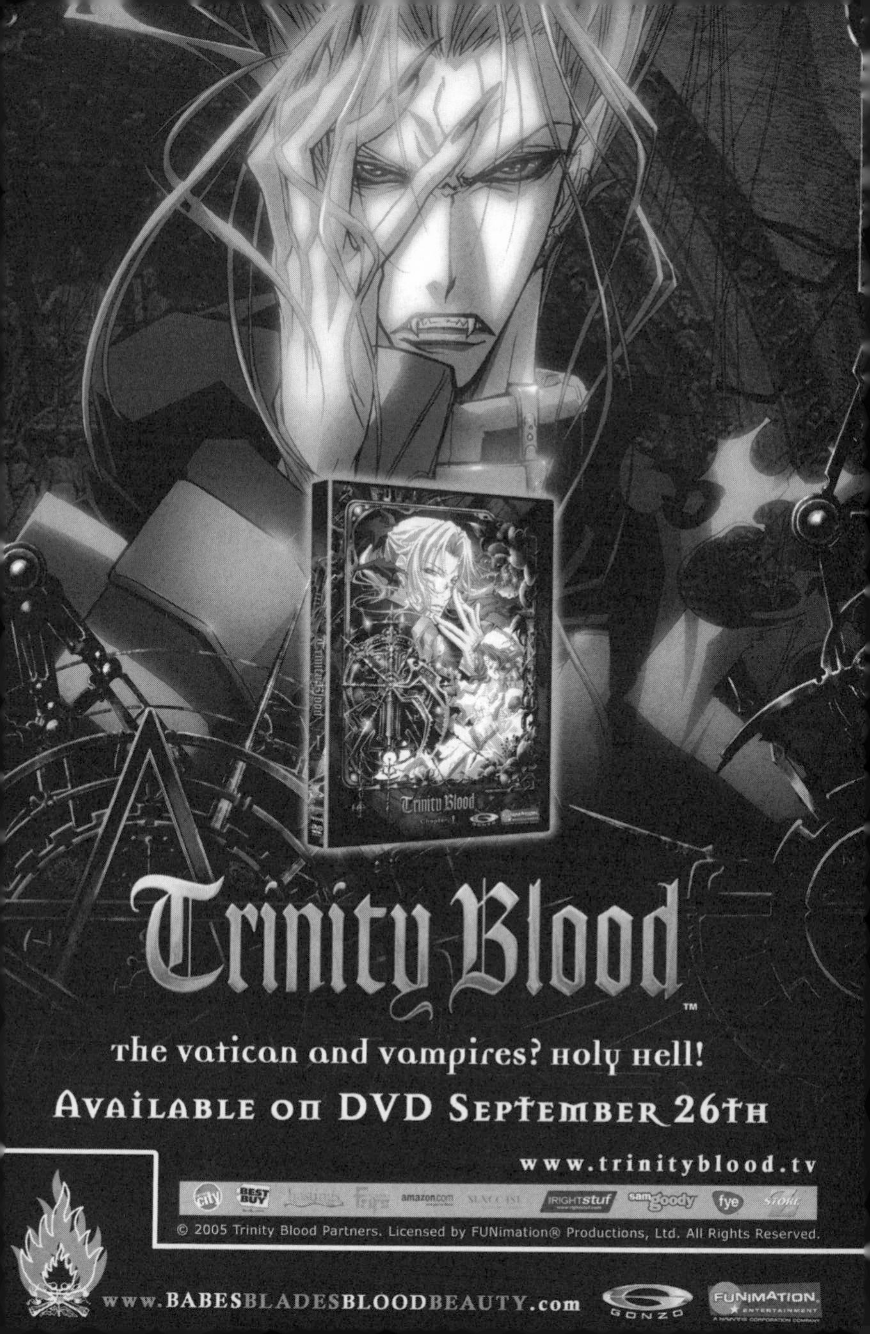
Trinity Blood
Trinity Blood
Chapter 1
Trinity Blood™
the vatican and vampires? holy hell!
Available on DVD September 26th
www.trinityblood.tv
© 2005 Trinity Blood Partners. Licensed by FUNimation® Productions, Ltd. All Rights Reserved.
www.BABESBLADESBLOODBEAUTY.com
GONZO
FUNIMATION ENTERTAINMENT

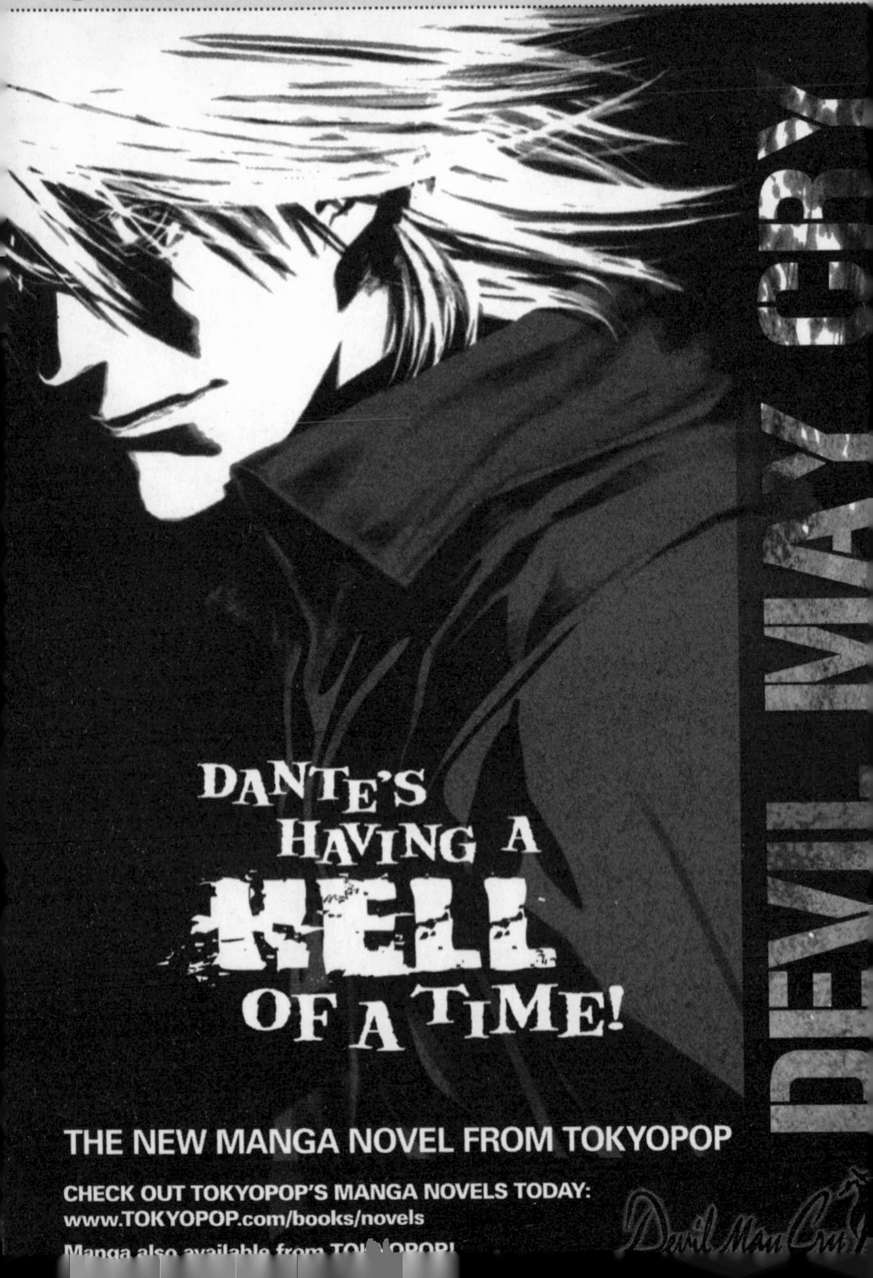
DEVIL MAY CRY
DANTE'S HAVING A HELL OF A TIME!
THE NEW MANGA NOVEL FROM TOKYOPOP
CHECK OUT TOKYOPOP'S MANGA NOVELS TODAY:
www.TOKYOPOP.com/books/novels
Devil May Cry

Check out the following series also available from TOKYOPOP Fiction:

www.tokyopop.com/popfiction

POP
FICTION